Praise f

"My first contact with Derek was during the MAPP when he presented on the concept of harnessing and controlling fear in mountain sports, and the delicate balance there can be between managing the real prospects of life-threatening danger and the exhilaration of the sport, the natural surroundings, and the complete, wonderful absorption of being in the moment. It was an incredible presentation, and later when I became his MSc dissertation supervisor on his project exploring flow and mindfulness, that same balanced and nuanced search to understand what both flow and mindfulness actually are was evident. The results of that research and exploration are in this book, where Derek outlines some of the intricacies of the flow and mindfulness experience often taken for granted or misunderstood, and how we can take control of our attention, train and hone it, to experience some of the best states of being that life has to offer, and to find that optimal 'zone' we all are striving to reach. With his customary respect for science, critical and questioning eye, Derek helps the reader explore the teachings of second wave positive psychology to help people find their peak lives, on or off the peaks".

–**Dr. Genevieve Cseh**, course co-leader, Buckinghamshire New University MSc Applied Positive Psychology, flow researcher

"This is a must-read for anyone interested in getting self-consciousness out of the way and to effortlessly (and effortfully) create the flow environment for self and others to flourish. Time well invested in gaining compelling and practical ways to learn, enjoy, flow and grow in life".
—**Bernadette Callanan**, learning, leadership and organisational development specialist

"Derek offers a roadmap for learning and having fun while doing so, with the purpose of helping us find greater satisfaction in our daily lives so increasing our mental wellbeing. Anyone interested in improving themselves and the quality of their lives will relate to this comprehensive and insightful book".
—**Sheelagh Lennon** (MIACP), counsellor and psychotherapist

"Derek has written a fantastic book for coaches and leaders encouraging you to understand some of the principles of positive psychology and to explore flow in your own environment. Derek uses plenty of examples within the book from coaching outdoor sports, however the theories that he uses will be equally at home in a business or personal environment. A highly recommended book for those coaching or leading in the outdoor environment".
—**Nancy Chambers**, outdoor instructor and author of the Daily Gratitude Journal: Write your way to better health and happiness

"Learning" or developing a skill involves a change in behaviour by the learner. By nature, we all learn differently. It may involve 'trial and error' for some, deliberate practice for others – but we all require appropriate and effective feedback to develop our skills further. After over thirty years of assisting individuals in that developmental process within a mountain environment, Derek has once again dovetailed his extensive, practical experience with contemporary thinking within the field of psychology – the result of which is the production of his latest book. Combining real-life observation, underpinned with the appreciation and appliance of science, the contents of this book will definitely assist you to develop your skills further.
–**Dougi Bryce**, Chief Executive Officer, JudoScotland

"I love Derek's writing style; it reads very well, and it feels personal. I also love how everything interacts and how well it is connected. The LEFG method is excellent and makes total sense".
–**Inge Beckers**, career & leadership coach and talent development specialist

"This book encompasses the coaching approach I have used with Dave Ryding over the last ten years and I thoroughly believe that this kind of method is essential for improving performance".
–**Tristan Glasse-Davies**, Dave Ryding's lead coach since 2010

"This book is engaging and fascinating, with Derek's thoughts and ideas flowing easily into each other and you find yourself thoroughly absorbed from the start. He has given me thought provoking methods with which to review my own coaching practice and develop ideas. Derek suggests a number of great ideas to work with, all of which equally apply to life as well as sports coaching. I can't pick one chapter or topic from the book as a favourite, as for me they are all linked together and take one on a journey of thought, reflection and review. A very valuable book to own".
—**Jane Campbell Morrison MBE**, sailing coach

"This book is a must read for any individuals that coach or work with people in the outdoors. It made me reflect on some practices that I take for granted and has made me understand my own mindset better. Maintaining well-being through physical activity in nature has always been important to me, but it is even more so in these times and this book helps immensely".
—**Marit van Kampen**, International Mountain Leader (IML) and secondary school teacher of IT and outdoor education

"Chapter 2 is a masterclass in how to use structured activity to develop performance. I really like Derek's Diamond model, Learning Zones and route to Mastery".
—**Hugh Monney**, director, British Alpine Ski & Snowboard School network

Learn, Enjoy, Flow & Grow

ALSO, BY DEREK N. TATE

Parallel Dreams Alpine Skiing

Ski Instructors Handbook: Teaching Tools & Techniques (co-authored)

Learn, Enjoy, Flow & Grow

Using the principles of positive psychology to help find passion and meaning in life

Derek N. Tate

PARALLEL DREAMS PUBLISHING

First published in 2020 by Parallel Dreams Publishing.

This edition published 2020 by Parallel Dreams Publishing, 90 Argyll Road, Kinross, KY13 8BL, Scotland, UK.

ISBN: 978-0-9556251-9-0 (print version)
ISBN: 978-0-9556251-7-6 (e-book)

Copyright © Derek N. Tate 2020

The right of Derek N. Tate to be identified as the author of this work has been asserted by him in accordance with the Copyright, Designs and Patents Act 1998.

All rights reserved. No part of this publication may be reproduced, stored in a retrieval system, or transmitted, in any form, or by any means (electronic, mechanical, photocopying, recording or otherwise) without prior written permission of the publisher.

Printed and bound by Kindle Direct Publishing or IngramSpark

Photo credits:
All photos taken by Derek or Shona Tate © Parallel Dreams

While the author has made every effort to provide accurate internet addresses and YouTube links at the time of publication, neither the publisher or the author assumes any responsibility for any errors, or for changes that are made after publication. Moreover, the publisher does not assume any responsibility for third party websites and their content.

Visit www.paralleldreams.co.uk/learning-hub to access all of the Parallel Dreams Coaching Academy resources. This includes many free documents and tools and a highly informative blog all of which support this book.

For Shona,
without whom none of this would have been possible,

and for my Mum & Dad
who have always believed in me and allowed me to
pursue my interests wholeheartedly.

Brief Contents

PART ONE – LEARN — 11

CHAPTER 1: Find your interests — 13
CHAPTER 2: Practice with purpose — 25
CHAPTER 3: Focus your attention — 51
CHAPTER 4: Learn mindfully and be curious — 71

PART TWO – ENJOY — 83

CHAPTER 5: Develop and nurture your passion — 85
CHAPTER 6: Enjoy the journey — 103
CHAPTER 7: Perform with creativity — 113

PART THREE – FLOW — 127

CHAPTER 8: Foundations are vital — 129
CHAPTER 9: Experience the characteristics — 145
CHAPTER 10: Flowing with mindfulness — 159

PART FOUR – GROW — 197

CHAPTER 11: Discover your purpose — 199
CHAPTER 12: Simply be — 213
CHAPTER 13: Find hope and meaning — 227

CONTENTS

PREFACE	xvii
INTRODUCTION – The importance of science within positive psychology	1

PART ONE – LEARN — 11

CHAPTER 1: Find your interests — **13**
- The psychology of interest — 13
- Knowing your strengths — 15
- Maintaining interest — 17
- Generalise or specialise — 18
- Don't be afraid to fail — 21
- Follow your bliss — 23

CHAPTER 2: Practice with purpose — **25**
- Purposeful & deliberate practice — 26
- Talent vs. skill — 34
- Burnout — 36
- Skill acquisition — 37
- Learning zones — 41
- The road to mastery — 47

CHAPTER 3: Focus your attention — **51**
- Attention — 51
- Focused attention — 53
- Training the skill of focused attention — 55
- Effortless attention — 58
- BEE Focused — 60

CHAPTER 4: Learn mindfully and be curious — **71**
- Mindfulness — 71
- Mindful learning — 76
- Curiosity — 81

PART TWO – ENJOY — 83

CHAPTER 5: Develop and nurture your passion — 85
- Human motivation — 87
- Intrinsic and extrinsic motivation — 88
- Passion, motivation and long-term goals — 89
- Exemplars of passion — 95

CHAPTER 6: Enjoy the journey — 103
- Process vs. outcome — 105
- Flexibility of your goals — 106
- Savouring the joys of the journey — 106
- Finding enjoyment even in adversity — 108
- Harnessing additional benefits — 111

CHAPTER 7: Perform with creativity — 113
- Defining creativity — 113
- Performing with creativity — 115
- Improving your ability to perform with creativity — 123

PART THREE – FLOW — 127

CHAPTER 8: Foundations are vital — 129
- A little history — 130
- Mental and physical? — 132
- F1: Clear goals — 133
- F2: Unambiguous feedback — 134
- Flow in creativity — 137
- F3: Challenge/skills balance — 138
- Task difficulty and environment — 140
- Interactions of the foundations — 142

CHAPTER 9: Experience the characteristics **145**
- C1: Focused attention — 147
- C2: Action-awareness merging — 149
- C3: Sense of control — 150
- C4: Loss of self-consciousness — 152
- C5: Transformation of time — 154
- C6: Autotelic personality — 155
- Flow inhibitors – a recap — 157

CHAPTER 10: Flowing with mindfulness **159**
- Synergy and contradictions — 160
- Del's research question — 161
- The study — 161
- Overall learning from my research — 182
- A proposed new model of flow — 188
- Foundations revisited — 190
- Team flow — 193
- Summarising flow — 195

PART FOUR – GROW **197**

CHAPTER 11: Discover your purpose **199**
- Purpose or calling? — 205
- Values based purpose — 208
- Self-actualisation — 209

CHAPTER 12: Simply be **213**
- Human being or human doing? — 214
- Mental health vs. mental illness — 215
- Ego and beyond — 217
- Self-transcendence — 220
- Ten ways to simply be — 221

CHAPTER 13: Find hope and meaning **227**
- What is hope? — 231
- Hope vs. optimism — 233
- Maintaining hope — 235

- The gift of hope 238
- Understanding meaning 239
- Meaning and positive psychology 240

EPILOGUE 243

REFERENCES 247

ACKNOWLEDGMENTS 267

INDEX 269

THOUGHT CLOUDS COLLATED 277

ABOUT THE AUTHOR 283

YOUR NOTES, THOUGHTS & IDEAS 284

PREFACE

This book that you are about to read has been written over the last year however, in reality, it has been a lifetime in the making. It is the culmination of my journey to date and is based on a series of chapters in my life some of which inevitably overlap.

At the end of the book I include some acknowledgements which are related more directly to the writing of this work, while this preface acknowledges people who have positively impacted my journey thus far.

The book itself is a mixture of my life and career with me recounting particular episodes, hence there is an autobiographical aspect to it. In essence, through a lifetime of being a learner, teacher and coach I have developed a 'coaching method' intended for you, the reader, to use for self-coaching and/or with those that you work with.

My journey is very much dominated by the sport of alpine skiing, but it is as much about my love of the outdoors and the mountains hence those who have contributed to the book (mentioned in the acknowledgements) are friends and colleagues with whom I have worked and come to admire.

The book is a combination of the aforementioned journey and my Masters in Applied Positive Psychology (MAPP) which I completed in 2019. Therefore, the coaching method is a synthesis of life experience and all that I learned, and reflected on, during the three years of the MAPP.

I am including a brief history of my journey, in this preface, not with the intention of boring you but simply to put some context around what unfolds in the pages that follow.

My skiing journey began with two school trips to Pamporovo, Bulgaria in 1983 and 84, a place I would revisit with the Irish Interski Team as Ireland's delegation leader in March 2019. My early skiing all took place on the artificial ski slope at Kilternan in County Dublin, which is owned and run by the Ski Club of Ireland (SCI). The next chapter saw me move to the Spey Valley in Scotland where I worked for Carrbridge Ski School being fortunate to have some amazing mentors/role models in the likes of Dougi Bryce and Alan McGregor.

I then moved to Châtel in the Portes du Soleil region of France where I worked for Ian and Jane McGarry. I developed a great friendship there with Andrew Smart who unfortunately left us far too early.

The 90s were spent based in Edinburgh and then more latterly the 'wee' county of Clackmannanshire. The PG Diploma Sports Coaching at Moray House was my first taste of academia and Hillend Ski Centre provided a great place for me to continue developing as a ski teacher and race coach with Lothian Ski Racing Association. Firpark Ski Centre in Clackmannanshire was my first 'employed' job and I took on the role of centre manager. It was also where I met, my soon to be wife, Shona.

PREFACE

Another great chapter was working on the East Coast of the USA with the recruitment of ski instructors for ski schools and delivering of performance courses the next challenge. Loon Mountain, Bretton Woods and Waterville Valley provided some great memories.

Then the lure of the alps beckoned again and this time it was Courchevel, in the Trois Vallées, where I worked for New Generation Ski School. This would also see me begin my time as a trainer and examiner for the British Association of Snowsport Instructors (BASI), while also continuing my role as Head of Education for the Irish Association of Snowsports Instructors (IASI) a position I held for 20 years!

Chamonix and the region of Mont Blanc was the next chapter. Here my wife and I took on the franchise of British Alpine Ski School Chamonix (BASS Chamonix) with Megève/St. Gervais being added a few years later.

The appeal of the big mountains has always been a strong part of my journey and over time I have come to love being in the alps in all seasons and not just winter. While this book is very much about learning, skill acquisition, positive psychology and well-being it has only come to fruition because my experience living and working in the outdoors has been made sense of by participating in the MSc Applied Positive Psychology. I truly believe that if you want to find passion and meaning in your life then this book has something to offer you. So, let me begin by helping you understand more about positive psychology, the science behind it and what my coaching method is all about.

INTRODUCTION

The importance of science within positive psychology

It would seem prudent to begin this introduction, and indeed book, by defining positive psychology and moreover, what it is and what it is not! The field (or subfield) of positive psychology came to the fore in the year 2000 when Martin Seligman and Mihaly Csikszentmihalyi published a paper titled "Positive Psychology: An introduction" (2000). This subfield has its roots in humanistic psychology and the work of eminent psychologists such as Abraham Maslow, Rollo May and Carl Rogers. Maslow's well-known hierarchy of needs, which was subsequently depicted in a pyramid (not by him[1]), is part of his human motivational theory (1943), moving from one's most basic needs; food, water, sleep etc. through safety, belonging and esteem needs to what he termed **self-actualisation**; in essence achieving one's full potential. This theory, with its final stage of self-actualisation, links beautifully with the title of this book and the aim of individual growth. Furthermore, as discussed below (and throughout this book), it is also an important part of positive psychology.

---

[1] Scott Barry Kaufmann (2020) in his book Transcend points out that "Maslow never actually created a pyramid to represent his hierarchy of needs" (p. xxviii).

INTRODUCTION

Positive psychology is the *scientific* study and practice of what makes life worth living. It focuses on the individual, institutions and society. Its aim is to improve the quality of life, bring more meaning to life and to prevent the kind of illnesses that can occur when life becomes barren and meaningless. A wide range of subjects come under the umbrella of positive psychology including strengths, emotions, mindfulness, flow, savouring, resilience, self-compassion, hope, meaning and wisdom.

The subjects deemed to be part of positive psychology have been studied and researched for many years (pre-dating the formalisation of this subfield). While much of the original research literature was derived from the USA this is no longer the case thanks, in part, to specific courses of study such as the Masters in Applied Positive Psychology (MAPP) being offered in many countries, and a course from which I graduated in 2019. As this subfield of psychology has matured it has moved beyond the narrow, and somewhat elusive, pursuit of happiness and began to embrace a more *realistic* view of a life worth living, recognising that life has many ups and downs and it is how people handle the bumps in the road that defines them. This led to the emergence of Positive Psychology 2.0 (PP 2.0) with books like, 'Second Wave Positive Psychology: Embracing the dark side of life' (2016) brilliantly capturing this evolving approach. I was fortunate to be taught by Piers Worth on the MAPP and to meet, at various conferences, Itai Ivtzan, Tim Lomas and Kate Hefferon who were the authors of the book. It is worth noting that PP 2.0 is much truer to the original humanistic psychology of Maslow, Rogers et. al, and it was pointed out by Scott Barry Kaufman (a modern-day humanistic psychologist) that the pursuit of happiness (a primary aim of early positive psychology) was never

INTRODUCTION

really its goal, but rather to realise one's full potential and find fulfilment through self-actualisation.

One of the criticisms levelled at the humanistic psychology movement was that it was not very scientific and lacked academic rigor and empirical research. In contrast, positive psychology has always been based around scientific research using quantitative and qualitative methods. While any science can be criticised, the very fact that there are findings to be discussed and tested adds weight to interventions that follow for many of the aforementioned *subjects* which come under the heading of this subfield of psychology; strengths, emotions etc.

Returning to the title of this introduction: The importance of science within positive psychology; the *importance* is that this book is science based and is grounded on sound principles from positive psychology together with my own research (as part of the MAPP). This is mixed with my own life experiences, which include a lifetime of participating and coaching in sport (primarily alpine skiing) and a love of the mountains and all they have to offer.

The book is divided into four main sections, which are based on the Parallel Dreams Coaching Academy's coaching method of **Learn, Enjoy, Flow** and **Grow** (LEFG), which also became the title of this book. This coaching method has evolved from our philosophy; **Learn it, Love it, Live it**, which I introduced to the Irish Association of Snowsports Instructors (IASI) in our build up to the World Interski Congress in Ushuaia, Argentina in September 2015. IASI adopted this philosophy, which was set out in detail in an e-book prior to the congress

(Tate, 2015). For a sports national training and certification body to 'adopt' such a philosophy means that they are putting both snow sports instructors and their guest's wellbeing at the forefront of everything they do. So, there is clearly a correlation between 'Live it' and 'Grow' in so far as finding something that you enjoy (in whatever domain), pursuing it to the point that it becomes a part of your life and adds to your overall growth as a person. But it is important to grasp that the LEFG coaching method is cyclical rather than linear (a point I will return to, and expand upon, as the book unfolds). You do not simply move from one stage to the other. There is some overlap with the stages e.g., while learning, you should also be enjoying the process. While in flow it is likely that you may enjoy the experience itself as well as feeling a sense of enjoyment afterwards. And some of the best learning takes place when you are in flow. Furthermore, learning, enjoyment and flow all lead to growth. But, arguably, most important of all is that you should keep experiencing **all** these stages throughout your life whether that is in one area of interest or many.

Each part of the book contains several chapters each of which begins with some questions for you, the reader, to ponder, either whilst reading the chapter and/or afterwards. Answering these questions will help you to reflect on your own life and to what extent you are applying, or indeed have applied, the LEFG coaching method. By engaging in this way, you have the opportunity, and perhaps even the permission, to choose how to move forward. My hope is that you will be inspired to learn something new, revisit something you used to enjoy, or put more time and practice into existing interests, which will ultimately result in further growth for

INTRODUCTION

you as an individual and for others with whom you engage.

Part one: Learn starts with a chapter that tackles the issue of finding your interests. It looks at how people may experience pressure from today's society, especially children, to find an interest and then specialise in that particular activity, from a young age, in order to become very proficient. But is it better to generalise and try lots of different activities and perhaps become just *good* in a whole range of areas? Or should all available time be spent practicing just one activity so that a high level of skill is attained? In addition to answering these questions the importance of knowing your strengths, maintaining interest and being allowed to fail are covered.

The old adage 'practice makes perfect' is discussed, in the chapter that follows, with the *quality* of the practice being centre stage. How can practice time be purposeful or even deliberate, and should it always be an enjoyable experience? Should practice sessions be easy or difficult and where do 'learning zones' and skill acquisition fit in? Within the context of this chapter the important talent vs. skill debate is also addressed.

Focusing your attention is a crucial part of the learning process and is covered in the next chapter. But what exactly is 'attention' and where should it be focused when learning a skill or activity? Does it depend on where you are in the process of acquiring that skill? Indeed, is 'attention' itself a skill and, if so, can you get better at it? How much effort should it take to keep your attention focused on a particular activity? Towards the end of this chapter a useful and innovative concept is presented to help you better understand how to focus your attention.

The final chapter, of part one, looks at learning mindfully. Mindfulness is very much in vogue in today's fast paced and stressful world. With the recent pandemic of Coronavirus mindfulness is being offered as a way of coping with the stress of the situation. But what is mindfulness and what does it mean to learn in a mindful way? Is this different to more traditional methods of learning? The way that you learn and the vital role that curiosity plays concludes not only this chapter but also part one of the book.

Part two: Enjoy begins with a chapter all about passion and what it means to be passionate about something and how that relates to enjoyment. Indeed, where does your passion come from and how do you nurture it? What do you do if you lose your passion? Should you call it a day and do something that gives you more enjoyment, or should you knuckle down and persevere? Human motivation is discussed, in some detail, by looking at whether goal attainment is extrinsically or intrinsically driven. This chapter concludes with some fantastic exemplars of passion giving you, the reader, a great insight into the lives of others and what is driving them.

Oftentimes when people attain their goals there can be a sense of disappointment, especially after the initial euphoria of completion. Hence, the next chapter is all about the journey and the importance of reminding yourself to enjoy it, and to savour it, by being more process driven than outcome orientated. After all, if you are going to invest so much of your time into what interests you then the reward and enjoyment need to be ongoing as you work towards your goal(s). This chapter also addresses the challenges that people face and looks at how the journey can (and will likely) include some difficulty. This is very much in line with how positive psychology has evolved; to embrace the negative with the positive, and, in the face of adversity, the contributor to this chapter is one of the most inspiring individuals you are likely to meet especially given all that he has and continues to achieve.

The last chapter of part two suggests that performing with creativity is beneficial to enjoyment, not least, because being creative links back to learning mindfully. This, in turn, can benefit skill development. But what does creativity mean, and can anyone be creative, or is this just for the chosen few? One of the fascinating aspects of this chapter is how five different people see creativity in their lives and in their chosen activities and their answers add a really rich perspective to creativity and performance.

Part three: Flow looks at the 'mental state' that is achievable when a person is fully engaged in the task at hand. Why is flow such a desirable state? Is it something that can be made to happen, or is it more elusive? Are some people more likely to experience it than others? What can inhibit flow from taking place? These and other questions are addressed by looking at the research that has been done in different areas of life including sport, and my own research with the sport of Alpine skiing.

In chapter 8, the three foundations of flow[2] are covered, in considerable depth, including how these can be controlled and manipulated, both by the individual looking to experience flow and a coach working with others who wish to achieve it. Moreover, you will consider the interaction of these three foundations and how understanding this further increases the possibility of facilitating flow both for yourself and your learners.

The six characteristics that people experience, when in flow, are covered in chapter 9. These experiences have been documented, via self-report, from many years of research. Do you always experience all of these characteristics? Can flow experiences vary in depth and frequency? These questions are discussed and answered, and the chapter concludes with a recap of the inhibitors of flow.

The third chapter, in this section, chapter 10, begins by looking at the potential synergy between flow and mindfulness, while also addressing perceived conflicts. I then dive into my research study covering the research question, the study itself, what was learnt (the results) and how this has led to a proposed new model of flow. This chapter then looks at 'team flow' (a much less researched area) before concluding with a summary of all three chapters.

---

[2] In Csikszentmihalyi's writings there are nine dimensions of flow and there has been constant debate about exactly which ones are foundations and which are characteristics. In this book, the nine dimensions are presented in chapters 8 and 9; three foundations and six characteristics, while chapter 10 reveals a 10th dimension, increasing the foundations to four, based on the findings of the author's master's research.

Part four: Grow is to some extent a result of the previous three parts of the LEFG coaching method. The suggestion is that for those who are open to learning, and who enjoy the process, and regularly find flow, that they will grow as individuals, become more self-actualised and potentially find their purpose or calling in life. Discovering your purpose is what chapter 11 is all about while stressing that purpose alone does not ensure growth and that it must be ethical and underpinned by good morals and values.

Part of growing is also about 'being' and not always rushing to do. So, the next chapter titled 'simply be' challenges you to spend more time being rather than doing. This, at the very least, redresses the balance between being and doing so that you avoid spiralling downwards towards mental illness and instead promote good mental health. Having a healthy ego is also considered within this chapter and how, by achieving this, you can again promote a healthy balance between being and doing. There are some important links back to earlier sections of the book, in this chapter, which help you to really understand the LEFG journey and how it connects together. This chapter then concludes with some practical ideas that you can use to bring more 'being' into your life.

Finally, the book concludes with a chapter about hope and meaning. How does hope manifest itself and how can you maintain it when life's challenges inevitably come along? Where does optimism fit in and how important is realism? One of the revelations of part four of the book, and in particular this chapter, is that hope and meaning, and ultimately growth, is not an individual pursuit. The involvement and support of others is vital and even more important is your ability to move beyond the self in the service of others. This then strengthens your meaning in life so that you are better prepared to respond to whatever life throws at you.

So, what you are about to read is a 'coaching method' that can be applied to yourself and others with whom you work. Ultimately, this is a process of self-development and if you are willing and open to learning, throughout your life, then you will give yourself the opportunity to learn, enjoy, flow and grow.

ARE YOU READY?

Hiking in the alps

PART ONE
LEARN

"The capacity to learn is a gift; The ability to learn is a skill; The willingness to learn is a choice."

Brian Herbert

CHAPTER 1

Find your interests

> Questions to ponder:
>
> ⇒ What are your interests?
> ⇒ Do you like to try *new* things?
> ⇒ Do you generalise or specialise?

To begin this chapter, it is useful to understand interest from a psychological perspective.

The psychology of interest

In positive psychology 'interest' is described as a positive emotion. Barbara Fredrickson lists it as one of the 10 forms of positivity and says, "when you're interested you feel open and alive" (2010, p. 43). So, it would seem that cultivating interest is a good thing to do, not least, because it leads to a positive emotional state.

Interest is something that you are drawn to, something that grabs hold of your attention and makes you want to explore and discover. There are a couple of key learnings from what I have just said. Firstly, as *interest* grabs hold of your attention, then it should follow that if you can maintain interest then you can remain focused (more on maintaining interest later in this chapter and on focusing attention in chapter 3). Secondly, as interest is something that encourages you to explore and discover, the coach or teacher should allow the student to learn in this way and use appropriate teaching tools and techniques!

Angela Duckworth in her excellent book 'Grit' (2016) highlights, discovery, development and deepening as being the three key elements for making an interest grow. So, let me unpack these three a little more;

Discovery: How often were you asked as a child, "what are you going to be when you grow up?" And, how often, as an adult, have you asked this question to your children, or relatives/friend's children? The problem with such a question is twofold as firstly, it places unnecessary pressure on the child to decide such matters and secondly, it potentially interferes with, or detracts from, their opportunity to explore and try out many different things. But, perhaps, even more importantly young children are unlikely to know the answer, as pointed out by Duckworth when she says, "childhood is generally far too early to know what you want to be when you grow up" (2016, p. 103).

Development: Time is clearly a factor when it comes to developing an interest. Exposure to that interest must happen over and over again. For instance, I did not start skiing until I was seventeen years old. But, in reality, I was already in love with the sport by the time I had my first lesson. Why? Because, as a child, I had avidly watched it on television, I was fascinated by the skiing scenes from James Bond movies such as 'The Spy Who Loved Me'. I loved everything about the alps and hence Geography was my favourite subject at school. And it was my Geography teacher who organised the school skiing trip when I was in fifth year. So, by the time I put skis on, for the very first time, I had already been exposed to the sport and its environment, on many occasions, and had developed a strong interest.

Deepening: The support and encouragement of others is an important factor when it comes to deepening an interest. This can come from a number of sources be it family, coaches, friends and peers. The more support you have then the more likely it is that your interest will deepen and last.

While the three elements above are, undoubtedly, crucial in making an interest grow, Duckworth also mentions that, "interests are triggered by interactions with the outside world" (p. 104). Therefore, people are clearly limited by their own particular situation, where they live, wealth (or lack thereof), opportunities in their community etc. When you read the stories of famous people, like Steve Jobs (Apple), Richard Branson (Virgin), Bill Gates (Microsoft), Jeff Bezos (Amazon) or even Nelson Mandela, it is clear that all of them were presented with opportunities and followed particular interests because of their interactions with 'their' world. Everyone will be presented with opportunities, but the important thing is to seize them when they come along.

Knowing your strengths
Strengths are another important part of positive psychology. But what have they got to do with finding your interests? And what exactly am I referring to when I mention strengths? Let me begin by answering the latter;

Strengths are in essence the things that people are good at (be it a practical skill, a behaviour, or aspect of character) and when you get the opportunity to use your strengths best performances normally follow. But there is more to strengths than simply performance, as is pointed out by Linley and Bateman (2018) who break strengths down into performance, energy and use. In other words, apart from performing well, using a strength should energise you, it should be something that you enjoy doing and you need to have, or be given, the opportunity to use it. Unfortunately, we are pre-conditioned to focus on the negative and on weaknesses. As a ski instructor I have often asked my students, at the start of a session, what they would like to focus on within the lesson and it is not uncommon for someone to say, "just tell me what I am doing wrong". It takes a real shift in their learning mindset to instead focus on what they are doing well and to build on those strengths. Linley (2008) sums this up nicely saying, "we succeed by fixing our weaknesses only when we are also making the most of our strengths" (p. 23).

When I was studying for my master's degree in positive psychology and I was introduced to strengths I was confused. Initially, all the focus was on aspects of character such as creativity, honesty, kindness, leadership, humility, gratitude etc. as depicted by the VIA Institute on Character (www.viacharacter.org). But there were other 'approaches' to strengths such as the CliftonStrengths (www.gallup.com/cliftonstrengths) and Strengths Profile (www.strengthsprofile.com) which were more directed towards the world of business and more work related skills e.g., drive, enabler, improver, listener, rapport builder etc. So, the language surrounding 'strengths' seemed to be incredibly varied and focused on character and behaviours and less about practical skills such as specific techniques in sport, or your ability to solve a difficult equation in maths. My confusion was resolved when I understood that strengths can in fact relate to all of the aforementioned, with the crucial point being that doing and learning certain practical skills will interest some people because they are getting to use their strengths of character or engage in behaviours that they enjoy. Therefore, if you know your strengths, and are given the chance to try lots of activities, then you will find that there is a link between using your strengths and the things that interest you most.

Maintaining interest

I already talked about *deepening* an interest and there is little doubt that this is part of maintaining interest. But there is more to it than just the support of others.

The *beginner* will find novelty in 'new' hence it is more likely to be interesting. While for the more proficient making progress or improving skill levels, however incremental, is vital for maintaining interest. And if you are a coach, then delivering sessions that are varied, and that cater for the individual and their needs, will be more likely to keep students engaged and consequently interested.

But feedback is also a crucial element in making progress. That feedback can come from others, most likely coaches and teachers, but also peers. However, intrinsic feedback is the most important source of feedback and if it is moment to moment then even better (as will be covered in part three; Flow). The good news is that learning to use intrinsic feedback is a skill in itself so you can get better at it.

Another important consideration for maintaining interest, that needs to be mentioned here and will also be expanded on in the section on Flow, is the level of challenge that the activity provides. Too little challenge can lead to boredom, while too great a challenge can result in fear. There needs to be enough of a challenge to stretch your skill level and provide some excitement.

Generalise or specialise?
There appears to be different schools of thought when it comes to acquiring expertise or mastery in any given domain. Essentially the debate moves between whether it is better to specialise and focus your time and energies on one thing? Or whether it is better to sample many different activities and take time to decide what really interests you?

For the *specialise* camp this pressure to decide quite often comes from parents and coaches who believe that the only way their children/students can acquire mastery is by starting as young as possible with the rational that the amount of practice time required to reach the top means that narrowing the focus to one interest is required. This is particularly relevant to the domains of sport and music. Personally, as a ski racing coach, I have witnessed this to the point that the parents are living out their own dream of success through their children. Perhaps some of this *pressure* has unwittingly come to the fore because of popular books like 'Outliers' by Malcolm Gladwell (2009) and Bounce by Matthew Syed (2010) which talk about the magic 10,000-hour rule (roughly 10 years) – the amount of practice time needed to achieve mastery in a given domain. This has, however, in my view, been misunderstood and I will expand on this point when discussing skill vs. talent in chapter 2.

The generalise camp appear to take a different view. David Epstein wrote a fascinating book all about this called Range (2016). Contrary to popular belief he points out that Roger Federer did not get serious about tennis until he was a teenager and played many different sports as a younger child. So, if, arguably, one of the best tennis players to ever lift a racket can leave specialisation until adolescence then this goes some way to dispelling the myth that to become the best in the world you must choose early about your interests.

Coming back to my own sport of skiing, I have watched the Carrick-Smith boys[3] with interest over the last few years. Their mother, Emma Carrick-Anderson, was one of Great Britain's best ever slalom skiers competing at

---

[3] The Carrick-Smith boys have their own Facebook page which beautifully depicts the range of sporting activities in which they engage https://www.facebook.com/carricksmithboys/

four Winter Olympic games. Their father, Phil Smith, also an accomplished ski racer was a leading figure within the British Association of Snowsport Instructors (BASI) for many years. So, it is hardly surprising that with this pedigree and opportunity that their three boys would become avid ski racers from a young age. However, what is different to many other children who begin a sport at a young age is that their parents have a philosophy that ties in very much with the message of the book Range in that they have been given the opportunity, and encouraged, to do many different, albeit complementary, sports. This has ensured that their interests are varied and many, while also developing crossover skills that help their primary sport. When I asked Phil about this, he summed it up this way, "skiing down every racecourse presents unique challenges every single moment of every single run. The key to success is to create, at subconscious level, infinitely varied responses to solve infinitely varied problems where nothing is ever the same. The only consistency is inconsistency itself. This in itself is a life's work". Hence doing many different sports aids this process.

But, perhaps, the definitive argument about generalising or specialising comes from Emilie Wapnick in her Ted Talk titled, "Why some of us don't have one true calling" (2015). In this talk she says that she is a multipotentialite meaning that it is OK to have "a range of interests and jobs over one lifetime". So, possibly it is OK to be just *good* at a whole range of activities because, after all, not everyone can be the best!

Don't be afraid to fail

Zig Ziglar said, "failure is an event not a person" (1997, p. 11) which is such a true statement. Yet for so many people 'failure' is seen only in a negative way which is sadly perpetuated by many corners of society. Ironically though when you read about, and get told, the stories of successful people the narrative nearly always includes how often these people have failed on their road to success. So why then does failure continue to carry such a stigma? Let me start by looking at a definition of failure. The Merriam-Webster dictionary includes, "lack of success" and "a falling short" both of which imply that you have tried and put forth some effort. The problem seems to be how this failure is perceived both personally and by others in society. In order to succeed you need to cope with your own self-doubt and with a lack of tolerance from others. Unfortunately, the latter is the biggest problem here as people tend to worry a great deal about what others think and are concerned with being socially labelled as a failure!

One of the biggest issues with this negative relationship with failure is that it can seriously impact your willingness to try new things and explore new interests. Yet if you could develop a more positive view of failure, based on learning from it, then being given that permission would greatly help with not only taking the risk to try new things, but also with maintaining interest through the development and deepening stages. This is why fostering a growth mindset can be so helpful in shaking off the stigma of failure.

Growth mindset: Carol Dweck, a world-renowned psychologist for researching achievement and success, across many domains, first published the book Mindset in 2006 in the USA and Great Britain in 2012. In this book she describes in detail differences between a 'growth mindset' and a 'fixed mindset'. Typically, someone with a growth mindset would see intelligence as something that can be improved and that personality – the kind of person you are – can be changed for the better. Conversely, a person with a fixed mindset would see intelligence and personality as traits that cannot be changed.

Thus, it is hardly surprising that someone with a fixed mindset would interpret failure as an identity e.g., I am a failure. Whereas, the person with a growth mindset would not allow failure to define them even though they may find the *event* to be a very painful experience.

A great example, from the world of sport, of someone who is a massive success, yet has had to deal with many failed events, is the British tennis player Andy Murray. In addition to many other tournament victories, he has won three Grand Slam singles titles including Wimbledon in 2013 and 2016, and the Olympic Gold for singles in 2012 and 2016. His 2013 Wimbledon victory made him the first British player to win the men's singles title since Fred Perry in 1936, while his Olympic achievements mean he is the only tennis player, male or female, to win two singles gold medals. However, Murray has had his fair share of disappointment having reached a total of eleven Grand Slam singles finals therefore losing eight of them including all five Australian Open finals. It would be fair to say that Andy Murray has, or has developed, a growth mindset.

FIND YOUR INTERESTS

The good news though is that you can change your mindset and if you have more of a fixed mindset you are not stuck with it. Focusing on passion, effort and commitment all foster a growth mindset, whereas fixed judgements such as, genius or loser move you into a fixed mindset. So, be very careful how you talk to yourself and others as interests are pursued.

Follow your bliss

Joseph Campbell famously said, "Follow your bliss. Find where it is, and don't be afraid to follow it" (1988) and I guess what he meant by that was that you should do what truly interests you, what you are good at, and therefore what utilises your strengths. So, it's more than just doing something that is exciting or fun, but rather something that is deeply part of you, and if it really is *part of you* then you won't be afraid to pursue it.

However, doing what you love and turning that into a lifelong interest, or your profession, or even a calling, is easier said than done. External pressure from family and friends can sometimes influence your decisions and not always in a supportive way. But why should you not have a job that you love?

Let me offer an example here from my own situation when I was coming towards the end of my time in secondary school, in Dublin and moving out into the world of work! This was 1984. It would be fair to say that I was not very academic and achieved very average grades in subjects like maths, English, economics etc. But I had always been interested in, and participated in, a variety of sports and in 1983, as I touched on earlier, I went on a school skiing trip to Pamporovo, Bulgaria. Over the next four years I became obsessed with the sport and practiced almost every day at the artificial ski slope at Kilternan, Co. Dublin.

Without going into too much detail, I subsequently got the opportunity, aged 20, to go to Aviemore and do a winter season as a ski instructor for Carrbridge Ski School, working on Cairngorm Mountain. I had truly found my interest and I wanted to pursue ski teaching as a career. But this was the 80s and I was a kid from Dublin, Ireland. Teaching skiing was certainly not a common career path, in fact, it was unheard of, and what always sticks in my mind is how some of my extended family, and family friends, commented that I just needed to *get it out of my system* and that I would eventually get a real job. Of course, the inference here was that something as enjoyable as being a ski instructor could not possibly be a real job because real jobs cannot be enjoyable – work should not be fun! Thank goodness I had the determination to follow my interest and can now look back at a ski teaching career of 34 years and counting.

Had I not engaged in such purposeful practice though none of this would have been possible and this leads nicely into chapter 2.

Alpine skiing

CHAPTER 2

Practice with purpose

> Questions to ponder:
>
> ⇒ Is your practice time purposeful?
> ⇒ Should practice time always be fun?
> ⇒ How much practice should you do?

How often have you heard the expression "practice makes perfect"? Or, indeed, variations such as "practice makes permanent", or "correct practice makes perfect"? Like many such well-intended sayings there are elements of truth, but also the potential for a good deal of misunderstanding. There is no doubt that in order to become proficient in anything you need a good deal of practice, but how much? And surely the quality of that practice is important? In this chapter, I will attempt to clarify exactly what it means to 'practice with purpose' and to dispel some myths about practice itself and issues such as talent vs. skill. I will also cover how practice relates to skill acquisition and learning zones while being aware of the potential for student burnout. Finally, I will put all of this together in mapping out a road to mastery for those who wish to achieve such levels in the activities that they do.

Purposeful & deliberate practice

Purposeful practice is structured, thoughtful and focused. Naïve practice is where something is repeated over and over hoping that the repetition by itself will somehow improve performance. A rather tongue in cheek saying that examiners of ski instructors would often say, when a student would return to be reassessed for a technical level and showing no change in performance was, "same skiing same result". And while that sounds a little bit harsh the truth is that quite often people are unaware of how to practice and therefore the time spent practicing is to some extent wasted, or, at the very least, not maximised. So, the *quality* and *structure* of the practice is just as important as the amount of time spent practicing.

Anders Ericsson[4], in his excellent book 'Peak' (2016), looks at the science behind expertise and suggests that effective, quality practice can be purposeful and deliberate with the latter, a phrase which he coined, being even better for those who wish to reach the peak within their given domain. The book is based on his own research including his original studies on violinists and pianists (Ericsson, Krampe & Tesch-Romer, 1993).

In his theoretical framework, Ericsson has identified several *requirements* for practice to be purposeful and deliberate. So, let me expand on the four requirements of purposeful practice (PP) and the further four requirements of deliberate practice (DP). In doing so I

---

[4] It was of great sadness to learn that K. Anders Ericsson the internationally renowned psychologist died on the 17th of June 2020 while I was writing this book.
See https://en.wikipedia.org/wiki/K._Anders_Ericsson for more info.

will include some examples from my world and people who, I believe, epitomise these ways of practicing. I will also see how Ericsson's framework fits with other experts from the field of teaching, learning, practice and the acquisition of skill.

PP1. Clear goals: Having specific, clearly defined goals is the first requirement for purposeful practice. To succeed in any area of life setting and achieving goals is a fundamental skill, and to make your practice sessions more productive having clear goals for each session is a very good idea. But what behaviour should follow the setting of goals? Larry and Hersch Wilson, in their book Play to Win (1998), say that goals, "can stretch you and inspire you, but goals are not ends in themselves, they are merely guideposts that point toward *personal best* performance" (p. 160-161). So, in essence, what they are saying is that your goals need to inspire you to push yourself and get outside of your comfort zone (see PP4 and Learning Zones for more on this).

The acronyms SMART & SMARTER are well known pathways for effective goal setting and achievement and have appeared in many books and articles over the years[5]. They stand for, Specific, Measurable, Achievable, Realistic, Time-phased, Exciting and Reward. I also wrote about these in the Ski Instructors

---

[5] It is generally recognised that George T. Doran was the first to present the SMART acronym as part of a management review article in 1981. The letters have varied slightly, in terms of what they stand for, and SMARTER is simply a development of the original idea that has been frequently used in management training with the E representing "Evaluate' or 'Exciting' and the R being 'Revisit/Revise' or 'Reward'.

Handbook – Teaching Tools and Techniques (Lockerbie & Tate, 2012).

PP2. Task focus: Focusing on the task at hand is the second element of purposeful practice and there is clearly some crossover here with, 'focus your attention' (chapter 3) and with one of the foundations of flow, 'focused attention' (chapter 8), not to mention a number of other chapters. But I make no apology for this as all discussions around this vital element contribute to a fuller understanding of how being able to focus your attention contributes to successfully navigating your way through the LEFG coaching method. But for now, I will simply note that focusing on the task at hand is paramount if the time spent practicing is to be effective.

PP3. Immediate feedback: The third element of purposeful practice is having ongoing and immediate feedback during the practice. Without feedback there is no way of knowing how you are progressing. Feedback can come from a number of sources with the most obvious being the feedback you receive from a teacher or coach. However, external feedback is of little use if you cannot develop intrinsic feedback such as feelings, sensations, kinaesthetic awareness and auditory. My focus when working with students is to help them to become more proficient at using these intrinsic sources so that they can *match* them against any external feedback they receive. A very common teaching style called self-check (see Mosston & Ashworth, 2002) is ideal for developing these feedback skills. Moreover, people who have good intrinsic feedback skills are able to measure their progress immediately while they are actually doing the task, and this is not only vital for practicing purposefully but also for achieving flow (see chapter 8).

PP4. Stretch yourself: The fourth and final requirement for purposeful practice is being able to get outside of your comfort zone so that you stretch your available skills. This is, perhaps, the most talked about element in practicing, skill development and learning. Daniel Coyle in his book 'The Talent Code' (2009) talks about the need to struggle as you learn so that you make mistakes and have to put in effort to correcting them while practicing. This ties in very much with the idea of stretching your available skills and working outside of your comfort zone (Jackson & Csikszentmihalyi, 1999). Coyle talks about this element being part of what he refers to as 'deep practice' but accepts that this is very similar to Ericsson's 'deliberate practice'. The only difference is that Coyle's deep practice includes neuroscience and the importance of myelin[6], while Ericsson is coming at it from the perspective of a cognitive psychologist hence focusing on the mental state.

What should become clear to you, the reader, as you progress through this book, is that there is a strong

---

[6] The Merriam-Webster dictionary defines myelin as, "a soft white material that forms a thick layer around the axons of some neurons and is composed chiefly of lipids (such as cerebroside and cholesterol), water, and smaller amounts of protein". Coyle focuses on myelination where the nerve fibres are wrapped in myelin, which "increases signal strength, speed, and accuracy" (p. 31) allowing our thoughts and movements to become faster, stronger and more fluent. This process is especially effective when practicing outside of your comfort zone and stretching your available skills.

relationship between some of the theories presented and reviewed. For example, the four requirements of purposeful practice have many similarities with the foundations of flow (see chapters 8 & 10). This, in itself, should accentuate their importance.

Deliberate practice according to Ericsson includes all four components of purposeful practice plus four additional requirements. Again, I have expanded on these below with some of my views.

DP1. Teacher/coach: The first requirement for making practice more deliberate is guidance from a teacher or coach. For me the word guidance is important as it stresses that the role of the teacher is to help and advise the student rather than impose fixed techniques. As a fan of the world of martial arts and its most famous son, Bruce Lee, I am reminded of his words, "a teacher is a pointer to truth, not a giver of truth" (2016, p. 90). In sport, where fundamental movement patterns need to be learned, a teacher ensures that functional movements are developed. As the student progresses the role of the teacher evolves to help the student move beyond fixed practice routines to experimentation and discovery of varied responses.

DP2. Rigorous training: Training methods that are rigorous and formal are the second requirement for deliberate practice. 'Nothing in life worthwhile comes easily', is the kind of advice your coach might give you and there is no doubt that rigorous practice may not always be fun, although you should do your upmost to keep your training fun by adding variety wherever possible. But because you are required to work outside of your comfort zone and at "near-maximal effort"

(Ericsson & Pool, 2016, p. 99) it's hardly surprising that practice time will sometimes be just hard work!

Mikaela Shiffrin is not only one of the best alpine ski racers, male or female, to ever put on a pair of skis, but she is a supreme athlete. At just 25 years of age she is potentially just reaching her peak, yet she has achieved more victories and accolades than most athletes do in their entire career. She has 66 World Cup victories to date across six disciplines including slalom, giant slalom, super-G, downhill, parallel slalom and alpine combined. She was the youngest skier ever to reach 50 World Cup victories and is fourth on the all-time list (as of February 2020), behind Ingemar Stenmark 86, Lindsay Vonn 82 and Marcel Hirscher 67. Shiffrin[7] epitomises hard work and deliberate practice and understands how important it is to use drills to develop performance, while always knowing exactly the purpose of that drill. She also knows the importance of transferring the skills developed in those drills into performance, which is very much the ethos of the IASI Skills Model (Tate & Kagan, 2018).

DP3. Developed field: The third requirement for being able to practice in a deliberate way is to have a well-developed field with people who have achieved mastery. Essentially having *expert role models* who have achieved a high level of proficiency in your domain greatly helps, not least with motivation for practice and belief that others (perhaps you) can achieve similar levels, but primarily by having an understanding of what these people actually do to achieve outstanding performance e.g., knowledge

---

[7] A great example of Mikaela Shiffrin's dedication to using drills to practice can be viewed at https://youtu.be/96VN_Brmnz0 and a little of the making of Mikaela https://youtu.be/9Q4aqi_cTA8

of what expert performance involves and looks like. These role models may be people that you know personally, or famous people from your domain that you admire.

Growing up I had a number of role models. Karate was my first really committed sport from age 11 and Bruce Lee was my idol. I would watch movies like 'Enter the Dragon' over and over (and even today still watch it). When skiing took over my life, I had many role models. Alan McGregor, a Scottish ski racer and coach from Edinburgh, was one of my first role models and teachers. He epitomised skilful, flowing, accurate performance and was a great role model because of his dedicated practice regime. The great Swiss ski racer Pirmin Zurbriggen, who won many World titles and the Olympic Downhill in 1988, was another mainly because he could win across all Alpine events from slalom to downhill (which, at the time, was quite rare). But, perhaps, the most exciting was (and still is) Glen Plake, the American extreme skier who came to fame in the iconic movie 'The Blizzard of Aahhh's'[8]. This opened up my mind to the possibilities of off piste and back country skiing and was one of the reasons I would later establish my ski school in Chamonix, France.

DP4. Mental images: The final aspect of deliberate practice is having refined mental images. These *images* which are representations of efficient and effective performance are built up over time and then transferred into reality. In sport these mental pictures come from a

---

[8] The Blizzard of Aahhh's was filmed during the winter of 1988 and the main portion of the film centred around the town of Chamonix and its major ski stations. https://youtu.be/aTsAsYmPgDk

combination of increased knowledge and understanding of expert performance e.g., being able to analyse those performances, plus seeing and feeling them. High level performers will have very sophisticated mental pictures of expert performance and will regularly integrate mental imagery as part of their practice.

When I train ski instructors, I frequently make them aware that they need to build their mental images over time and should therefore incorporate *performance analysis* into their regular training. This can be done in a variety of ways such as watching other performers while riding a ski lift, simply standing at the edge of the piste and observing other skiers, or analysing video of high-end performance.

All eight requirements for practicing with purpose, that I have discussed, are both logical and based on studies of more than 20 years. As touched on earlier the studies carried out by Ericsson, Krampe and Tesch-Romer (1993), on violinists and pianists, concluded that "the differences between expert performers and normal adults reflect a life-long period of deliberate effort to improve performance in a specific domain" (p. 400) and supported their theoretical framework for deliberate practice.

But a recent meta-analysis carried out by Macnamara, Hambrick and Oswald (2014) looking at all the major domains in which studies had been carried out on deliberate practice concluded that while it is important it might not be as important as has been claimed. Nonetheless, it would still suggest that structured, quality practice is the most effective use of time and best approach to becoming more skilful. But what is skill and is it different to talent?

Talent vs. skill

Before getting into the talent vs. skill debate it would seem useful to look at a couple of definitions.

One of my favourite comes from Scott Barry Kaufmann who says, "instead of treating talent as an 'innate ability', with all the knowledge and skills fully present at birth, I think talent is more accurately defined as a *predisposition and passion to master the rules of a domain*" (2013, p. 247). I think this beautifully emphasises that what we are born with can be developed through practice. Interestingly Daniel Coyle says, "we'll define *talent* in its strictest sense: the possession of repeatable skills that don't depend on physical size" (2009, p. 28). This suggests that in order to possess those skills, and therefore **be talented**, some effort has been expended i.e., practice!

So how come there is so much public perception that talent is born and that possession of it is down to luck. It is as if talent and genius are something mystical or divine – a gift from on high. This is not to say that everyone is born equal but this incessant message that is perpetuated by society is not helpful. Just take a look at the headlines in newspapers that say things like "incredible or amazing talent" or "overnight success" when referring to musicians or sporting stars. Or shows like "Britain's got Talent" or "The X-Factor" all of which pedal the idea that talent has been discovered and magically come out of nowhere. But, feasibly, the most damaging is when parents say things like "she's so talented" when referring to either their own children or other people's children. Remember that growth and fixed mindsets are fostered by the language that is used when praising someone, so being told that 'you are just so talented' infers that you have not had to put in the effort and commitment. While saying it about others provides the excuse that because they are lucky there is nothing you can do to match their gift so why bother trying.

But there is a plethora of writers who suggest that talent is not just down to innate abilities and is more to do with practice and skill development. I have already covered Ericsson's deliberate practice and Coyle's deep practice in some detail, but other writers who convey a similar message are Malcolm Gladwell in his book Outliers (2009) and Matthew Syed in his book Bounce (2011). What is common across all these writings is the assertion that to reach mastery, in any domain, requires around 10 years or 10,000 hours of practicing with purpose. Indeed, chapter 2 in Outliers is titled "The 10,000-hour rule" and Gladwell says, "Ten thousand hours is the magic number of greatness" (p. 41). However, such phrases are potentially misleading and can be easily taken out of context because they say nothing about the *quality* and *structure* of that practice, which is an integral part of Ericsson's research and one of the underlying messages of this chapter.

To sum up this debate I would say that genes, opportunity and skill are all part of the mix when it comes to becoming talented. Genes are what you are born with and will certainly influence whether you can become a jockey or be a successful basketball player. Opportunity comes from the environment in which you live and the people you are around. While skill is something that can be improved and developed through practicing with purpose. So, no matter who you are, or where you live, if you seize the opportunities that come along and engage in purposeful practice you can get better.

Genes, opportunity and skill are all part of the mix to becoming talented.

Burnout

One of the concerns about too much practice is the potential for burnout[9]. Such an occurrence is far from uncommon in sports where children have started at a very young age and been rushed into competing a lot, as well as undertaking large amounts of practice. I have personally witnessed this in alpine ski racing where excellent athletes have simply got fed up and lost all their passion. But I have also seen it in the world of ski teaching where instructors have been consumed by training and exams to the point where they fall out of love with the sport. Of course, other issues can come into play here such as the structure of the profession and the difficulty of earning a living wage!

---

[9] The Merriam-Webster dictionary describes burnout as, "exhaustion of physical or emotional strength or motivation usually as a result of prolonged stress or frustration"

Dave Ryding is Britain's most successful alpine slalom ski racer. In 2013 he won the season-long Europa Cup title, (the tier below World Cup), being the first British skier to achieve such a feat. He has placed second on two occasions in the World Cup, in slalom at Kitzbuhel in 2017, and in parallel slalom in Oslo in 2019. In a webcast hosted by Disability Snowsport UK (DSUK)[10], on the 14th of April 2020, Dave talked about how he was a relative late starter and that he was not even good enough to make it onto the British children's ski team. He emphasised how practice needed to be fun and that being at the top of the sport when you are 12 is not much use if you are not there when you are 25. When he placed second at the World Cup in Kitzbuhel he was 31 years old. This is testament to the idea that you need to take time to develop your interests and then practice with purpose with the quality of such practice being of paramount importance.

Skill acquisition

During my career in teaching snow sports I have been lucky to have worked with, and learned from, some of the great thinkers and practitioners of our domain. Hugh Monney is one of those people. Hugh, a pioneer of 'British ski teaching', created and leads the most successful network of elite snow sports schools in Europe: the British Alpine Ski & Snowboard Schools

---

[10] DSUK are a charity organisation who help people with disabilities use snow sports to transform not only their disability, but their entire lives. The webcast mentioned was one of several organised during COVID-19 'lockdown' to help create engagement, raise awareness of the charity and the work they do.
https://www.disabilitysnowsport.org.uk

(BASS)[11] and he has been a leading figure in the development of technical and teaching ideas for the British Association of Snowsport Instructors (BASI).

I asked him to expand on what he meant by, "the development of your performance depends upon your ability to get out of your own way and work with the learning process" (2010, p. 236). What he said was, "Learning can be challenging and uncomfortable. Some people take to it more easily than others. For example, *denial* is a natural reflex that's designed to save us the trouble of changing, when presented with new information. But, if we want to learn and develop, we need to change". So, this really emphasises the 'cognitive dissonance' that learning creates where you may have opposing ideas that conflict – that which you already know and the new information that is being presented. Part of the process of practicing means that you need to be willing to make changes as you practice and resolve these differences.

Skill acquisition, in itself, is a huge topic and many book chapters, articles and even complete books have been dedicated to this. The goal here is to present a model of skill acquisition, that I have developed, and then look at how practicing relates to each of the stages through 'learning zones'.

I introduced the **Diamond Model of Skill Acquisition** (DMSA) in June 2018. This model (see Figure 1) is an amalgamation of my ideas about the theories of flow (Csikszentmihalyi, 1975, 1990, 1997b), mindful learning

---

[11] The BASS Ski Schools operate in a number of resorts in the French Alps. For more info visit www.britishskischool.com

(Langer, 1998, 2000) and the original work on skill acquisition and stages of learning by Fitts and Posner (1967). As a trainer and examiner for BASI from 2003 – 2015 I was already very familiar with the work of Paul Fitts and Michael Posner as it formed the backbone of BASI teaching and learning materials. During my time on the Masters in Applied Positive Psychology (MAPP), 2016 – 2019, I immersed myself in the work of Mihaly Csikszentmihalyi and flow and also the ideas of Ellen Langer on mindful learning and the DMSA is the result of all this experience.

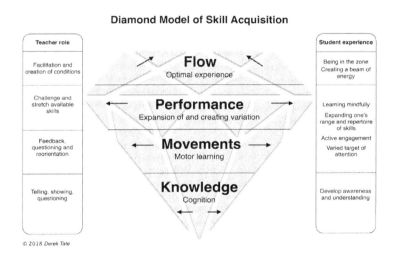

Figure 1.

A detailed explanation of the DMSA is contained in my June 2018 paper, and in chapter 14 of the IASI manual (2018a), so I will only briefly summarise my thinking behind the model in this chapter. Combining mindful learning (see chapter 4 for more on this) with flow theory from positive psychology, and Fitts and Posner's original stages of skill acquisition, creates an innovative model that puts the nurturing of student well-being as a desired outcome alongside the acquisition of skill. Facilitating flow for students not only creates enjoyment, in the short term, but it also develops a sense of achievement and a stronger self-concept, in the long term, and therefore is an integral part of the 'grow' phase of the LEFG coaching method.

There are couple of key aspects worth highlighting here;

Firstly, the significance of the model's *diamond* shape which emphasises that as the learner progresses through the first three stages of skill acquisition there is an increase and broadening of mental and physical abilities in relation to knowledge, movements and performance. Then in the third stage performance is refined and if conditions are optimal the performer may enter the flow state and narrow their focus towards their desired goal.

Secondly, the model incorporates both what the learner is likely to be experiencing, at each stage, and the teacher's role. This is very helpful for both parties, as the student can better understand the learning process and the frustration and struggle that may come when practicing, while the teacher better understands how to structure the practice sessions depending on where the learner is in relation to acquiring the skill.

As was highlighted earlier, at the outset of this chapter, quite often people are unaware of how to practice so the DMSA is a useful tool for both the student and the teacher in this regard and understanding and using learning

PRACTICE WITH PURPOSE   41

zones (which follows) provides another tool for enhancing the structure and quality of those practice sessions.

Learning zones

The idea of learning zones is not new and if you do an internet search you will find many images and articles about them. But the most common portrayal is of three zones called comfort, stretch and panic. My conceptualisation is different. It contains four zones; preparation, comfort, stretch and flow (see Figure 2) and they work beautifully with the stages of skill acquisition in the DMSA, and with how to practice in a purposeful way.

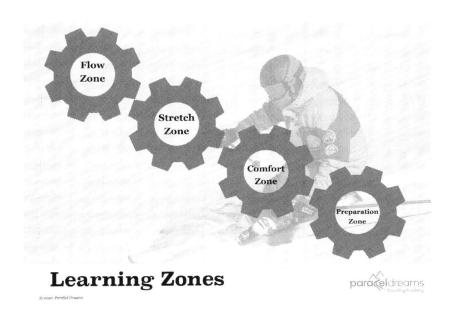

Figure 2.

Although my background is in sport, and particularly alpine skiing, these 'zones' can be applied and will work well with other domains. Before looking at each learning zone and how each one integrates with the DMSA and effective practice, it should be noted, that while the zones are depicted as a linear process, the learner will, in reality, move from one zone to the other in any given practice session. Both the student's level of skill and the desired outcome of the practice session will determine which zone is most appropriate and useful. My course leaders on the MAPP course, Dr. Piers Worth and Dr. Matthew Smith would regularly say, "trust the process", so knowing that, as a learner, you will move between zones helps you to embrace the struggle and accept the frustrations that are a part of learning.

Preparation zone: The preparation zone is just as it sounds – it is where the learner gets ready for the practice session ahead. In this zone the teacher has the opportunity to set a climate conducive to learning, while the student can clarify the session goals (PP1). This is where the 'learning contract' is established between student and teacher.

Of course, a teacher or coach will not always be present, but if guidance from a coach is being provided (DP1) then this could be sought prior to the session if required.

In this zone the learner will quite possibly be taking on board new information or clarifying understanding e.g., the knowledge stage of the DMSA.

Using my time at University as an example, where I attended one taught weekend per month, with the rest of my cohort, we were always encouraged to do a good deal of background reading and to listen to specific lectures online, as *preparation,* so that by the time we all came together we would be primed for the discussion that would follow and this was where the real learning took place.

Comfort zone: When practicing in different zones there is a constant interplay between using available skills and the environment. Some sports, like skiing or team sports e.g., soccer, hockey, basketball etc. are 'open' in the sense that the external environment is constantly changing. Whereas, a free throw in basketball, or throwing the discus in athletics would be more 'closed' as they are *less* affected by the external environment.

In every practice session it is important that the learner experiences periods of 'comfort' e.g., using their available skills in an environment that is relatively easy, not least because this will build confidence, facilitate warm up and allow for revision of skills that are already present.

But it is the comfort zone (environmentally) that is ideal for learning new skills or movement patterns, hence this is where motor learning takes place and where immediate feedback can be more easily received (PP3). It is also where the task focus (PP2) can be directed towards the movements of the body (more on this in chapter 3).

In the context of skiing, this would mean that the learner initially performs tasks that they have previously done on terrain that is relatively easy. They would then set about learning new skills where the environment remains friendly. A mantra that I always say to ski instructors that

I am training is, "don't change both the drill and the terrain at the same time. Just manipulate one variable at a time". But moving beyond the comfort zone is crucial for performance development, as too much time spent there can lead to boredom and reduced motivation due to the lack of appropriate challenge and, in sports like skiing, the thrill and excitement of stretching yourself (PP4).

Finally, the comfort zone also provides an ideal environment for honing and refining skills. In other words, developing accuracy. One of my favourite sayings is that "speed masks accuracy". In skiing anybody can go fast, if they have the confidence, as that's just gravity! But slowing things down increases the difficulty and requires accurate application of movements and excellent balance. It also helps with developing more accurate mental images of the performance (DP4). Daniel Coyle (2009) explains it this way, "going slow helps the practicer to develop something even more important: a working perception of the skill's internal blueprints – the shape and rhythm of the interlocking skill circuits" (p. 85).

Paradoxically, however, speed can also be your friend because it can create greater fluency and better timing of movements. This is where guidance from a coach (DP1) is very useful in helping you to know when to speed it up and when to slow it down (I'm sadly reminded here of Buck's Fizz's entry to the 1981 Eurovision Song Contest – Making your mind up).

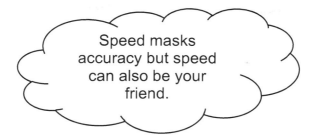

Speed masks accuracy but speed can also be your friend.

Stretch zone: The stretch zone is where performance is challenged. Learning good technique or sound fundamental movement patterns is vital as new skills are developed, but the learner then needs to have these skills tested in some way. This is why the stretch zone beautifully aligns to the performance stage of the DMSA. It is at this stage that the learner is creating "infinitely varied responses" (as Phil Smith said in chapter 1) thus creating variation in how those skills are applied. In physical activities this can include the rate, range and distribution of the movements and in open sports like skiing, where the external environment plays such a massive role, this variation of how the movements are applied is combined with changes in terrain and different snow conditions. This helps explain why 'open' sports are so complex and why a purely technical focus with a limited application of the movements would hamper the ultimate performance.

As mentioned at the outset of learning zones the structure is NOT linear. The learner will constantly move between zones and in particular between the comfort and stretch zones. There are several important points to note here. Firstly, the comfort and stretch zones (unlike the flow zone) are completely within the control of the learner and the coach to manipulate. Task difficulty can be varied, and the environment can be changed. Secondly, varying the intensity and type of training during practice helps with maintaining task focus (PP2) and increases or maintains enjoyment thus ensuring that rigorous training (DP2) can be done. Thirdly, in domains that have a developed field of experts who have achieved mastery (DP3) there will be plenty of examples of the type of training methods that they have employed and there is little doubt that they will include working in these different zones.

Flow zone: Getting into the flow zone is a desirable goal because having such optimal experiences (mentally) is enjoyable during and after the activity. Performers often talk about the buzz associated with experiencing flow and none more so than those who perform to live audiences e.g., musicians and athletes. Performers who experience flow on a regular basis can enhance and deepen their learning, create a sense of achievement and develop their self-concept. Being in flow is an immersive and intense experience and can become addictive – once you have experienced it you want more of it. There will be much more on this in parts three and four of the book. Suffice to say, in relation to the flow zone, while desirable, it can be elusive and there are no guarantees of reaching it. While it is a good place to *be* there will be many times in the learning process where it is not appropriate because more effortful concentration and greater mindful awareness is required (see chapter 4).

PRACTICE WITH PURPOSE

In summing up this section, Figure 3 shows how these zones map across to the DMSA.

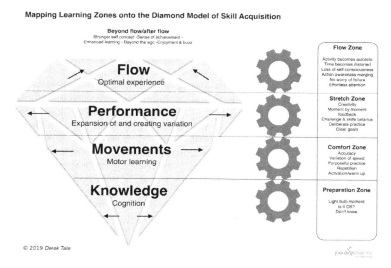

Figure 3.

The road to mastery

While genes and opportunity play their part, what is clear from this chapter is that achieving mastery, in any domain, takes a lot of time, effort and above all sophisticated, quality practice i.e., to practice with purpose. Figure 4 pulls together Ericsson's requirements of purposeful and deliberate practice and presents a pictorial model of the road to mastery.

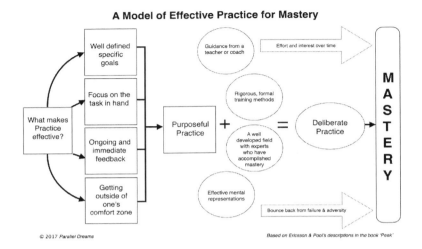

Figure 4.

It is worth pointing out, however, that mastery itself can vary and is not necessarily the same *level* across all activities. There are a number of factors that can influence this including the complexity and structure of the domain. For example, many musical instruments are very challenging to learn and master with one of the most difficult being the violin. And picking up on one of Ericsson's earlier mentioned requirements for deliberate practice, the need for a well-developed field with experts who have achieved mastery, it would be fair to say when looking at sports that they vary considerably in terms of how well-developed they are, not least, because of the varying worldwide participation. Sports like modern pentathlon, or equestrian events like dressage have very low numbers participating compared to athletics track events or alpine skiing. Access, popularity and cost may

PRACTICE WITH PURPOSE

well be the reasons for these differences, but the point here is that some sports are more well-developed with a greater number of experts who have achieved mastery. Ironically, in the UK (and perhaps other countries too) public perception is that the Olympics is the pinnacle of sport and that winning Olympic gold is the ultimate in mastery. However, World Championships, in many sports, are often more competitive and include a greater number of the world's best athletes because entries, from individual countries, are not limited by a quota system.

But, whether your goal is to reach 'mastery' in sport, music, physics, mathematics, biochemistry etc., or to simply become accomplished, in your domain, there is no doubt that you will need to focus your attention in the right way which is what the next chapter is all about.

Mountain biking

CHAPTER 3

Focus your attention

> Questions to ponder:
>
> ⇒ What is attention?
> ⇒ Is it possible to improve attentional focus?
> ⇒ Effortful or effortless attention?

Before addressing the question of how to focus attention when learning I will look at what 'attention' is in the context of this book, which is essentially about learning (mental and physical), mindfulness and flow.

Attention

So, let me begin with a nice simple definition, from the Merriam-Webster dictionary, which says that attention is, "the act or state of applying the mind to something". The words 'act' and 'applying' infer that to pay attention is an active process of *doing*. While the word 'state' is more a way of *being*. So, it appears that attention can be either intentional, or more a condition of readiness.

Aidan Moran, a cognitive psychologist and director of the psychology research laboratory at University College Dublin (UCD), is well known for his work on concentration in sport. He talks about there being three different types of attention (1996). Firstly, the ability to use mental effort to concentrate, or focus, on a particular target or piece of information. For example, how often have you been reading a book and got halfway down a page only to find that your mind has wandered, and you have no idea what you just read? In this instance you have lost concentration from the intended target of your attention. Interestingly, he refers to this first type of attention as "a highly valued practical skill" (p. 39) which is important as it implies that attention can be trained. It is a skill that can be improved with purposeful practice!

Second, attention can be spread across or divided between several different things. An example of this in skiing would be where an instructor is skiing behind their student and observing their performance, while also being aware of other skiers and snowboarders on the piste. Because the instructor is so well practiced at skiing, they can spread their mental resources across 1) skiing, 2) analysing performance and 3) awareness of other slope users. Conversely, a novice skier might be so focused on making their turns that they have no attentional resources left over to focus on the terrain, choice of route or other slope users.

And thirdly, attention can be described as being ready or alert. In the case of danger this would cause a heightened state of readiness for whatever action might be necessary.

Mihaly Csikszentmihalyi (2002) describes 'attention' as "*psychic energy*" (p. 33). What emerges in consciousness is a result of where attention is focused and everything that appears there (from the multitude of potentially available information) is processed by the energy of attention. Focusing attention, intentionally, can therefore be thought of as a "beam of energy" (p. 33) homing in on a specific target. Csikszentmihalyi, like Moran, also mentions that through **training** each person will learn to select the pieces of information that are relevant to them and the domain in which they are working.

"Psychic entropy" (2002) on the other hand refers to "disorder in consciousness" (p. 36) where there are distractions from the intended target of attention. In domains such as music or sport where there is pressure to perform, perhaps in front of a large audience or competing against others, then such distractions can be many (and unwanted). This reinforces why training the skill of attention is vital for all phases of skill acquisition as set out in the DMSA in the previous chapter.

Clarification – for the sake of simplicity when I refer to 'concentration' or 'focus/focusing' I will consider them to be interchangeable and relating to the **action** of paying attention.

Focused attention

Were you ever told at school (or, indeed, when learning anything) to pay attention? The reality is, that as long as you are conscious, you will always have your attention focused on something. The issue, however, is, when it comes to learning, whether your attention is focused on the appropriate cues or information.

Focusing your attention involves effort – mental effort, and this is especially true when learning something new.

But you also need to know what to focus your attention on. That's why teachers use a combination of explanation and demonstration to help their learners understand what to focus on before they have a go and imitate the performance. But they also need to know where to focus their attention when actually *doing* the activity (more on this later in BEE Focused).

Mind-wandering: A wandering mind is not helpful when attempting to learn something new. But, is a wandering mind always a bad thing? And what about daydreaming?

Scott Barry Kaufman and Carolyn Gregoire in their 2016 book "Wired to Create[12]" talk about "mindful daydreaming" (p. 42), which may sound like something of a contradiction but, in essence, is a type of mind-wandering. Their premise is, that in order to be creative, daydreaming is necessary as it gives "the mind space to dream, fantasize, and simply roam free" (p. 43), thereby promoting creative thinking.

However, Matthew Killingsworth and Daniel Gilbert (2010) carried out a study with around 5000 people, from 83 different countries using a smart phone app, to sample, in real time, throughout the day, their thoughts, feelings and actions as they carried out their daily activities collecting almost a quarter of a million samples. They then analysed samples from 2250 adults who were asked to rate their level of happiness, answer what activity they were engaged in, whether their mind was on that activity and if not whether their thoughts were

---

[12] Scott Barry Kaufman and Carolyn Gregoire share their thoughts about their book in a 92nd Street Y interview
https://youtu.be/sy3yhPD-F2k

pleasant, neutral or unpleasant. They found that not only did people's minds wander frequently, but that people were generally less happy when their minds were wandering.

As with many things in life it is about 'balance'. To keep attention intentionally focused, on a specific target for long periods of time, would be hard work and not necessarily what you want to do. Much better to be able to focus your attention when you need to e.g., when learning a new skill, practicing a drill, or performing in a high-pressure environment, and then allow the mind time to relax and roam free. Jonathan Schooler and colleagues (2014), in a chapter titled "The middle way: Finding the balance between mindfulness and mind-wandering", seem to concur with this line of thought by concluding "that mind-wandering can be a major detriment to cognitive performance and well-being, yet it may also enable future planning, facilitate creativity, and at least on occasion provide uplifting stimulation" (p. 25-26). They further suggest that training techniques should be developed so that "when the situation demands attention, one may be able to learn to spontaneously maintain focus on the task at hand; however, when task demands are more lax, mind-wandering can be indulged without fear" (p. 26).

Training the skill of focused attention
So, given that learning new skills requires focused attention that is intentionally directed at a specific target, how do you go about improving this skill?

Mindfulness: The chapter that follows will cover mindful learning in more detail and indeed, what mindfulness is all about. Therefore, in this chapter I will simply give a couple of examples, firstly of a research study that looked at the relationship between mindfulness and flow including the specific dimension of focused attention, and secondly how with my own research I developed a sport specific mindfulness training programme to improve the skill of focused attention with the aim of creating more flow experiences.

In 2014 Stuart Cathcart, Matt McGregor and Emma Groundwater measured the relationship between facets of mindfulness (see chapter 4 for more on mindfulness) and dimensions of flow (see chapters 8, 9 & 10), including focused attention, using highly validated questionnaires for both mindfulness and flow. The study involved 92 elite level athletes from a variety of sports, including team and individual. In support of their hypothesis they found a positive relationship between 'focused attention' and a number of the facets of mindfulness; 'describing' (putting words to internal experiences), 'acting with awareness' (which is about attending to activities happening now as opposed to behaving mechanically while focusing on something else), and 'non-judging of inner experience' (trying not to evaluate thoughts and feelings). They suggested that developing these aforementioned facets through mindfulness training could improve the skill of focused attention.

Mindfulness based skiing specific intervention (MBSSI): During my time on the MAPP course, and as part of my research study and dissertation (Tate, 2019d),

I created a mindfulness training programme for skiers[13], initially aimed at ski instructors with the primary goal of making better use of the time spent on ski-lifts e.g., drag lifts, chair lifts, gondolas, cable cars etc.

The design of this training programme concentrated on developing the skill of 'focused attention' during the time that skiers spent riding the ski-lifts (ascending).

The programme comprises of two broad mindful training areas; five **mindfulness meditative** activities and five **mindful communication** activities. Skiers riding the lift by themselves, or wanting to be in their own space, use the meditative activities, while skiers riding with others, be it friends/colleagues or strangers, use the communication activities.

Central to the design of the MBSSI was the edited work of Itai Ivtzan and Tim Lomas (2016) on mindfulness in positive psychology, and Rebecca Shafir (2003) on mindful communication and listening. I also identified a lack of such sport's specific mindfulness training programmes, especially for sports such as alpine skiing.

The overall reason for this mindfulness training programme, and the basis of the research study, was to increase the likelihood that the participants would experience flow when practicing and performing on the slopes (descending) because their 'focused attention'

---

[13] The MBSSI training programme is freely available via the Parallel Dreams Coaching Academy's Learning Hub (Documents and Tools). It comprises of two PDF files #1 Mindfulness Meditative Activities & #2 Mindful Communication Activities plus audio recordings of the meditative activities. www.paralleldreams.co.uk/learning-hub

skills had been improved. But much more on this later, including the results, in part three of this book: Flow.

Effortless attention

I have already referred to focused attention requiring mental effort when learning something new. So, in fact, it could be called 'effortful attention' especially when differentiating it from what is known as 'effortless attention'.

Arne Dietrich (2009), a cognitive psychologist and neuroscientist has developed a theory called 'transient hypofrontality' or THT which, while sounding rather convoluted, really boils down to the idea that, as you narrow your attention to the specific task at hand, and providing you are well practiced at that task, your attention becomes effortless. This is because a skilled performer requires less mental energy to replicate a task. So, from a skill acquisition perspective, if you are learning a new skill (knowledge/movements phases of the DMSA – see chapter 2), your attention will not only be focused but effortful. This requires you to process information through the 'explicit memory'. Skilled performers, on the other hand, use 'implicit memory' meaning the skill is more automated (performance and flow phases of the DMSA).

Let me take a step back, however, to clarify what I mean by explicit and implicit memory.

Explicit memory: This is where the learner consciously (and with mental effort) recalls known information from memory based on previous experiences, events, knowledge or concepts.

Implicit memory: This is where the learner is in the more automatic phase of learning and is able to perform a task using past experiences without having to consciously think about them. Limited attentional resources (energy) are not as much in demand and can therefore be diverted to other cues. Driving your car, or cycling your bike, would be good examples of activities that use implicit memory as you do not need to think through all the actions involved – you just do them – while placing your attention on the road or track ahead.

Figure 5 shows how, during the acquisition of skill, focused attention can be divided into effortful attention (using explicit memory) – for learning a new skill, and effortless attention (using implicit memory) – for skills that are well practiced.

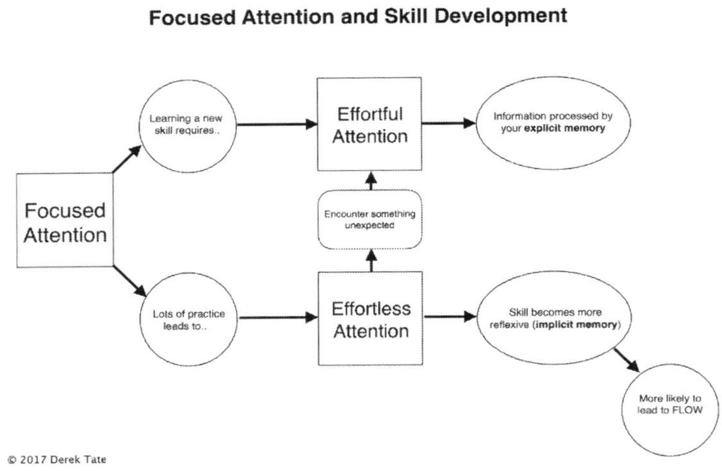

Focused Attention and Skill Development

Figure 5.

Two important aspects are;

1) Should the learner encounter something unexpected, e.g., the task becomes more difficult in some way causing their skill level to be over challenged, then they would revert to more effortful attention.
2) Effortless attention can lead to, or at least increase the likelihood of, the learner experiencing flow.

BEE Focused

In the autumn of 2019, I introduced the concept of BEE Focused, via the Parallel Dreams Coaching Academy blog and covered the idea, in detail, in my 10th of

FOCUS YOUR ATTENTION

November post titled, "Focus of attention in sport: Internal or external?" The model presenting the notion (see Figure 6) depicts a skier and while the concept works particularly well with alpine skiing, in reality, it works equally well with any activity where movement is involved, and motor learning takes place. To that end, I will look at the domain of music, in more depth, later, with the help of a friend and colleague who is a professional musician. But to begin I will focus on the domain of sport.

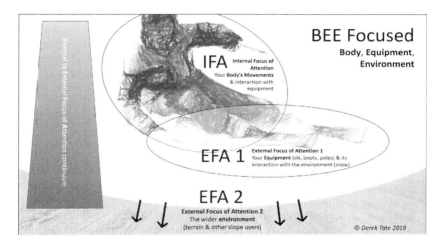

Figure 6.

Earlier in this chapter, when discussing focused attention, I raised the question as to where the learner should focus their attention when actually *doing* the activity?

The answer is that it will vary depending on the sport (individual, team etc.) and on the individual's level of skill e.g., knowledge, movements, performance, flow – DMSA. It should also be understood that this idea has implications, not just for the learner but, for the teacher as well and I will expand on this as I present the detail.

The idea for BEE Focused came about as I was writing my dissertation and reading many different texts about 'attention'. Gabriele Wulf and Rebecca Lewthwaite's chapter in the edited book Effortless Attention (2010) was of particular interest. They looked at a growing body of research evidence which suggests that using an external focus of attention enhances movement effectiveness and efficiency and can even speed up the motor learning process itself. Moreover, their suggestion is that by using an external focus (EF) rather than an internal focus (IF) of attention, that the attention itself will be more effortless helping to create flow zone conditions and potentially flow state for the learner/performer.

What is surprising about Wulf and Lewthwaite's examples is that an 'external' focus is largely one where attention is targeted at the equipment being used, by the participant, rather than the wider environment in which the activity is taking place! This led to my idea that, in effect, there are *three* levels of attentional focus moving from a very internal focus (movements of the body) to a more and more external focus (equipment and then the wider environment). This, in turn, led to the birth of the BEE acronym (see Figure 6 from earlier) which stands for Body, Equipment and Environment, with the body being the internal focus, the equipment being the first level of external focus and the wider environment being the second level of external focus. I will look at each of these in turn, in relation to alpine skiing, and then include some examples of how this works with other sports.

Internal focus of attention (IFA): This is all about the movements of various parts of the body and on how the learner focuses on them. In skiing this will include things like; balance/pressure points along the length of the feet (ball, arch, heel), opening and closing of the ankle joint, leg/foot turning, the path of the hips through the turn transition, the degree of leg lean and how the upper body counter balances to create lateral separation, rotational separation between the upper and lower body etc. This is by no means a comprehensive list of where attention can be directed, but highlights some common areas covered by ski instructors when working with their learners (apologies for the slightly ski related technical language but ski instructors reading this will know what I mean).

For me, there are two key points about using an IFA with skiers; firstly, that I spend proportionally more time getting my learners to focus on areas of their body that are close to their equipment (boots and skis) and secondly, that I get my learners to focus more on the 'active' rather than the 'passive' movements e.g., the active movements of turning the legs/feet as opposed to the more passive relationship of the upper body. The reason for this is because it encourages greater understanding and awareness of how the movements interact with the equipment, which I believe is essential during the movements (motor learning) stage of skill acquisition (DMSA).

External focus of attention 1 (EFA 1): It is this part of the research, compiled by Wulf and Lewthwaite, that really grabbed my attention (if you will pardon the pun). In spite of my extensive background in teaching alpine skiing, I had not really differentiated between, for example, focusing on tilting the skis on and off their edges with say rolling the feet, or feeling for the big toe on the outside foot and the little toe on the inside foot. While all these elements are clearly connected the research suggests that directing the learners' attention to the tilting of the skis (EFA 1) is better, from a skill acquisition perspective, than focusing on rolling the feet onto the big toe and little toe (IFA)?

The skiing research example that Wulf and Lewthwaite gave related to measuring amplitude and frequency on a ski simulator, with the largest results coming from focusing on exerting pressure onto the wheels (under the outer foot; EFA 1) compared with exerting pressure with the outer foot (IFA). This may seem like a subtle difference, but it got me really excited about ski teaching in the 2019/20 season and I have enjoyed seeing the impact of these subtle attention shifts with my learners and I am keen to experiment further (post COVID-19 pandemic!). For me, the jury is still out on whether such small changes in where the learner focuses their attention impacts their movement effectiveness and efficiency, or indeed speeds up the process of skill acquisition, but it has definitely made me, as a teacher, be really clear about where I want my learners to place their attentional focus for each task/run.

What is also very important when using the EFA 1 is that there is a clear link to EFA 2, hence the learner needs to be aware of how their equipment is interacting with the environment – the snow and then the terrain e.g., skis being deflected across the line of momentum creating skidding, or skis being tilted onto their edges allowing the shape of the skis (side-cut) to carve an arc in the snow etc.

It is also worth mentioning, at this point, that the learner's limited attentional resources will often be divided between an internal and external focus meaning they will be focusing internally and externally at the same time. But as the skill becomes more acquired and automatic their attentional focus will be directed more and more externally, allowing the movements to happen unconsciously and resulting in the attention becoming more effortless.

External focus of attention 2 (EFA 2): The wider environment in skiing (and snow sports generally) will include variance in the terrain (e.g., rollovers, cambers, changes in steepness, moguls etc.), other slope users, obstacles (e.g., rocks, trees etc.) as well as different snow types (powder, crud, groomed, ice etc.) and different weather conditions (sunny, poor visibility, wind etc.). It is hardly surprising then that snow sports are classed as an open skilled sport where the external environment places a great deal of challenge on the learner. Therefore, it is crucial for the learner and teacher to work in partnership so as to get to a point where more of the attentional resources can be directed externally. Tasks for encouraging this kind of attention will include skiing varied but constant corridor widths, using different turn shapes and varying the speed (requiring carving, or skidding, or a mixture), and then blending these together using funnels or hourglass type corridors. Being able to easily focus on these external cues, while maintaining a high level of the desired performance outcome, is a sure sign that motor learning has reached the acquired phase.

It also encourages more effortless attention, which in turn can lead to flow state when performing.

Other sports: So how does BEE Focused work with other sports?

When making a pitch shot in golf, the IFA could be the swing of the arms or the placement of the feet. The EFA 1 could be the swing of the club or the club head's contact with the ball, while the EFA 2 could be the path or flight of the ball, or the target e.g., the green or the flag.

During a free throw in basketball, the IFA could be the wrist movement, the EFA 1 the ball and the EFA 2 the hoop (target).

While serving in tennis the IFA could be the movement of the hand/arm to throw the ball, the EFA 1 being the height the ball is thrown to and/or the racket making contact with the ball. While the EFA 2 could be the net, the lines of the service box on the court or the opponent.

When I think about sports such as motor racing it seems obvious that in order to compete in a race the driver needs to be focusing almost exclusively on EFA 2 (the track and other cars) rather than EFA 1 the controls, or IFA the movement of the hands/arms! I have been fortunate to have attended the Grand Prix de Monaco Historic on several occasions and observe the driver's skill at handling cars, from different eras, on the street circuit of Monte Carlo. There is no doubt in my mind that those drivers are not only focusing on EFA 2, but their attention is narrowed like a beam of energy to the track ahead of them and sustained. This is undoubtedly a skill that is developed over time.

Other domains: So, what about other domains such as music?

Danny Ward, aka the Moodymanc, is a professional performing musician, producer and recording artist with over 30 years' experience. He has taught and studied in one to one and group situations, facilitated workshops and masterclasses and lectured from beginner to post graduate levels. He is also a qualified alpine and adaptive snow sports instructor and has been a practicing skier for over 40 years. I was really interested to get his perspective, as a musician, on the idea of internal and external focus of attention and this is what he said:

> "The process of learning, teaching or practice as an instrumental musician can describe a very similar experience to that of the skier in terms of 'internal' and 'external' focus. We are using a combination of 'equipment', 'environment' and 'physicality' to aim to achieve or experience a desired outcome. Within this process we might choose to focus distinctly on the internal (physical) input, or the 'external' equipment (musical instrument, or perhaps microphone in the case of a vocalist) and the environment (the acoustic properties of the space) in which we 'perform' in order to achieve this desired outcome. The dynamics of these relationships can be ever changing in the process of 'achievement', and distinct focus can be defined between internal and external throughout, whilst ultimately becoming a 'blend' in the overall experience. The conscious awareness and decision of defining the focus between that of internal or external factors however can have a distinct influence on our

experience of understanding and achievement. As musicians we have an ultimate focus on the 'goal' of directly 'influencing' our environment, and the way that we and others around might experience it. This is a consistent 'focus' throughout our process and in many ways might be described as a constant 'external' focus. This might not retain the same value whether 'performing', 'practicing' 'learning' or 'teaching'. Is this the same in skiing? (I'm enjoying my own process of understanding in this respect!)".

What is clear from Danny's comments is that the same three levels of focus exist; IFA – physical movements, EFA 1 – equipment (instrument) and EFA 2 – environment (acoustic sound for both the performer and others listening). It also appears that where that focus is directed is constantly changing yet the external seems to be of paramount importance. The question of whether the division of attention changes, depending on whether the musician is learning, practicing, performing or indeed, teaching, is probably yes in that once again the more accomplished the performer the more that the attention can be constantly external. I would also concur that I too am still very much learning and understanding and that is the eternal fun of both being student and teacher.

What has been clear from this chapter, I hope, is that *what* you choose to focus your limited amount of attention on is important, as is *where* that attention is placed – the target of your attention be it internal or external. The good news, once again, is that you can get better at it because focusing your attention is a skill and, just like a Formula 1 racing driver, you can develop the skill over time by practicing with purpose. One of the ways of training your attentional skills is through mindfulness practices which in turn can help you to learn in a more mindful way and that's what the next chapter is all about.

Grand Prix de Monaco Historic

CHAPTER 4

Learn mindfully and be curious

Questions to ponder:

⇒ What does it mean to be mindful?
⇒ What is mindful learning?
⇒ How will you benefit from learning mindfully?

Before looking at 'learning mindfully' and relating it back to aspects discussed in the previous chapters it is important to know and understand what mindfulness is and also what it is not!

Mindfulness

Throughout my lifetime I have been aware of how language has had its in-vogue phrases and words, at different points in history, many of which have become rather irritating! Today this would include words like 'bespoke', 'extraordinary' (incessantly used by people in the south of England and presenters on BBC breakfast), and of course 'furlough', which I have to confess I had never heard of before the current pandemic. But my point is that 'mindful' and 'mindfulness' are very much in this category and it seems that people just love to drop the word *mindful* into general conversation as if it sounds like they are being more considerate or even seem more educated. However, it also perpetuates misunderstanding around what the term is actually referring to.

It is hardly surprising then, that given my feelings towards the term, that I was a little sceptical of mindfulness within positive psychology when I began my journey on the MAPP course. But that very much changed and before I tell you why let me take a step back and clarify what mindfulness is and its origins.

Mindfulness meditation: There are many forms of meditation of which mindfulness is one. Other popular meditation practices include, loving-kindness, chakra, vipassana, transcendental, body scan, mantra etc.

The meditative practice of mindfulness has its roots in Eastern religions and Buddhist teachings. Jon Kabat-Zinn (1994) has been largely credited with popularising the practice in Western society and it has now become an integral part of positive psychology (Ivtzan & Lomas, 2016) with its goal of helping to promote well-being and human flourishing.

Kabit-Zinn's definition of mindfulness (1994) is about how you pay attention with the first requirement being that it is "on purpose". The second requirement is that attention is "present moment" and thirdly, that it is without judgement or as he puts it "non-judgemental" (p. 4). The 'present moment' aspect links beautifully with what has been discussed in the previous chapter, on 'focusing your attention', and also aligns to flow state and its foundational requirement of focused attention. 'On purpose' means that paying attention is an intentional act and that it is directed towards something such as the breath. This supports the idea that being purposeful about where you place your attention is a skill that can be practiced and improved. Finally, without judgment means there is acceptance to what is happening in the present moment; to what is being experienced, without getting caught up in a train of thoughts that might take you into the past or the future.

But does the practice of mindfulness mean that you have to meditate? The simple answer is no. One of my favourite definitions of mindfulness comes from Itai Ivtzan, during the video presentation no. 3 on the Mindfulness-Based Meaning Program, as "any moment when the activity and your mind are one" and "when we bring the activity and mind together" (Ivtzan & Russo-Netzer, n.d.). So, while there is little doubt that practicing more formal mindfulness meditation has many benefits, not least developing the skill of focused attention, mindfulness can easily be incorporated into your everyday life with any activity that you are doing, even the most mundane such as washing the dishes or brushing your teeth. It can also be brought to how you communicate with others, which was a major part of my own training programme (e.g., the MBSSI mentioned previously). For example, do you really listen when you are having a conversation with your partner, or a friend, or are you caught up in thinking about what you want to say in reply causing you to miss some key aspects of the conversation?

Misconceptions about mindfulness: Inge Beckers (2020) a friend and colleague from the MAPP course at Bucks New University wrote a blog titled, "Mindfulness is more than hype" and beautifully describes what it is, and what it is not, in simple and easy to understand language. One of the points that she makes is that it is not "thinking about nothing" and this is something that I have always stressed when I hear people say things like mindfulness is about emptying your mind! This could not be further from the truth as mindfulness is about maintaining your focus of attention on one or a number of things and is very much about bringing order to consciousness as was mentioned in the previous chapter.

The cognitive approach: While Kabat-Zinn is credited with bringing the Eastern version of mindfulness to Western society Ellen Langer, a professor of psychology at Harvard University, is credited with the "Western Approach to Mindfulness" (Ivtzan & Hart, 2016 p. 13). Langerian mindfulness is described by Itai Ivtzan and Rona Hart as being a cognitive process that is concerned with both mindfulness and mindlessness and how these two differing states impact a person's performance. Langer (1997) says, "a mindful approach to any activity has three characteristics: the continuous creation of new categories; openness to new information; and an implicit awareness of more than one perspective" (p. 4). She contrasts this with mindlessness where the person remains on auto pilot for extended periods of time and is therefore unable to attend to new information or stimuli. She is highly critical of 'learning' which takes place through a lens of mindlessness thereby rendering the practice time as less than useful because the skills may be overlearned and limited in their application even when the situation requires variation. But more about this shortly when I look at mindful learning.

Going back to my earlier point about what changed my mind about my scepticism towards mindfulness can be summed up as *sports psychology*!

Mindfulness and sport: As I began to study the construct of mindfulness and read many texts and research papers, I realised how much it was being effectively used within sports psychology. As the MAPP course continued, I was especially drawn to the work of Amy Baltzell, Director of the Sport Psychology Specialization at Boston University, George Mumford, renowned mindfulness and meditation teacher and Amy Saltzman, long-time athlete and mindfulness coach.

Baltzell and colleagues (2014) developed the Mindfulness Meditation Training in Sport (MMTS) programme, which was subsequently published in detail in the book 'The Power of Mindfulness' (2017), which she co-authored with Joshua Summers. This programme, which has been revised and updated to MMTS 2.0, provides meditation training specially for athletes aimed at improving their focused attention skills. Not surprisingly this programme was of great interest to me and a great comparison with the programme that I had developed for alpine skiers; the mindfulness-based skiing specific intervention (MBSSI) as mentioned in the previous chapter.

George Mumford's inspirational book 'The Mindful Athlete' (2016) covers his own struggles as an athlete and with drugs, and how meditation subsequently changed his life for the better. As a meditation teacher he has worked with some of the great names in American sport including Michael Jordan, Shaquille O'Neal and the late Kobe Bryant.

While Amy Saltzman's 2018 book, 'A still quiet place for athletes' provides, what is in effect, a practical workbook of mindfulness skills aimed at helping athletes find flow in both sport and life. Interestingly, I did not discover this particular text until after my own research study had been completed and I was in the process of writing up my dissertation!

Apart from enjoying reading and learning all about the positive impact of meditation and mindfulness within sport from the many available sources, including the aforementioned, what was particularly pleasing was that it validated my own work and that of the MBSSI.

Mindful learning

During the MAPP course my main focus was on the meditative aspect of mindfulness and how it can be used to not only compliment other sports psychology tools but specifically to help develop focused attention skills. But I have been equally interested in 'mindful learning' and how it fits into existing learning and teaching strategies that I have become very familiar with over the years and this was the reason I incorporated it into the Diamond Model of Skill Acquisition (DMSA; see chapter 2).

Ellen Langer (1997, 2000) who I mentioned a little earlier has a background in teaching and learning and has written extensively about learning in a mindful as opposed to mindless way. In her book 'The Power of Mindful Learning' she highlights a number of pervasive myths which she says *negatively* impact how people learn. These include; learning the fundamentals so well that they become automatic, and when paying attention that it must be to remain focused on one thing at a time. So, let me deal with each of these in turn.

Learning the fundamentals: Langer's assertion that learning fundamentals to the point of automation negatively impacts people's learning seems to contradict some of what has already been spoken about, particularly in chapter 2, in relation to practicing with purpose and skill acquisition. Therefore, let me try to resolve this perceived conflict.

In one of my blog posts (February 2020) I spoke about 'function vs. form' and asked the question; what is the best approach to learning a sport? In the context of this article *function* referred to learning via a 'skills-based system' while *form* referred to a 'manoeuvre-based system'.

A skills-based system is about developing a 'range and repertoire of skills' (see the DMSA student experience) that allow for "infinitely varied responses to solve infinitely varied problems" (see chapter 1 – Phil Smith's quote). As previously mentioned, open skill sports like alpine skiing with its constantly changing environment requires the performer to have this versatility. Hence the fundamental movement patterns need to be learnt in a way that develops range, rate and distribution. Range meaning the amount of movement, rate referring to the speed of the movement and the ability to vary it, and distribution being the timing of those movements. But I would assert that there is still a case for learning these movements and responses to a point of automation so that attention can be directed elsewhere e.g., external focus – equipment and environment (see previous chapter). Thus, Langer is partly correct especially if a limited set of fundamentals are learned to the point of automation without the ability to vary the response.

Conversely, a manoeuvre-based system focuses on replicating a form. In sport this would mean imitating a prescribed image quite often shown, or demonstrated, by a teacher. It would be wrong to simply discount this approach as *reproducing* good technique demonstrated by others has its value particularly early on in the motor learning process. Of course, this does not allow for individual variation (everyone is different – size, shape etc.), or environmental factors, but it does help to develop an initial set of sound movement patterns and in more closed skill sports this can be very helpful. It is also worth remembering that one of Ericsson's requirements for deliberate practice (chapter 2) was the development of sophisticated mental images and this is the result of increased knowledge and understanding of expert performance which, in part, come from 'observing' others.

Learning mindfully, therefore, goes hand in hand with a skills-based system, but it would seem to be a beneficial part of any skill acquisition process because it raises the individual's level of internal awareness and allows for more intrinsic feedback of performance. John Arnold, a good friend, mentor and coach, studied mindfulness and mindful learning at the University of Aberdeen and in his master's thesis (2013) found that "a heightened awareness of what was happening, internally, during performance was an overarching result of the intervention" (p. 62). His study focused on developing motor skills and performance with alpine skiers through mindful coaching strategies. He also concluded that "learning was productive rather than re-productive and the information which was used to shape performances originated with the learner and not with the 'model performance' provided by the coach" (p. 62). Mosston and Ashworth's teaching styles[14] (see Lockerbie & Tate 2012) support the idea that coaching strategies can be *reproductive* (styles A to E; p. 49) or *productive* (styles F to K; p. 50). The reproductive styles, to some extent (certainly styles A & B), align to the manoeuvre-based system, while the productive styles fit with a skills-based system as they allow the learner to discover for themselves and to problem solve. But once again, I would assert that there is a balance to be found here as all of the teaching styles are valid in certain situations and the skill of the teacher is to be able to vary the strategies and ensure that a mindful learning approach is incorporated whenever possible. Therefore, it could be said that mindful learning requires a mindful teaching approach where the teacher varies the strategies to suit the individual and their level of skill acquisition!

> Mindful learning requires a mindful teaching approach where strategies are varied to suit the individual.

---

[14] In addition to the reference noted in the text Mosston and Ashworth's Teaching Styles are very clearly described on www.spectrumofteachingstyles.org

Target of attention: Langer's other myth that I mentioned is that when paying attention that it must be on one thing at a time. Once again this may appear to conflict with earlier discussions (previous chapter) where it was mentioned that attention is intentionally narrowed to focus on a specific target from the multitude of possible stimuli and information available.

However, Langer's point actually builds on, and enhances, what I have already discussed, in the previous chapter, in that she says that children, and indeed adults, are regularly told to pay attention without any investigation of what that actually means. When asked what paying attention means most people think that they need to *fix* their attention on one stimulus. So, there appears to be a perception that as you narrow your attention to a specific point that attention is then held *rigidly,* whereas in reality the target of attention should vary. For example, if you were to look at a scenic landscape in a photo, and concentrate your attention on the scene, your eyes would continuously scan the photo noticing all the detail of the picture. Langer (1997) sums this up nicely when she says, "successful concentration occurs naturally when the target of our attention varies" (p. 40) and this idea is captured within the DMSA where it is suggested that the 'student experience' during the movements and performance stages of skill acquisition should (among other things) include a varied target of attention.

Moreover, Langer goes further by saying that "varying the target of our attention, whether a visual object or an idea, apparently improves our memory of it" (p. 42). This is based on studies she and colleagues have conducted one of which related to different groups reading short stories while travelling by train. The mindful groups were asked to think about different endings and to change several aspects of each story including reading them from different viewpoints. The focus groups were asked to home in on three or six specific features of each story but not change anything about the stories. While a control group simply read the stories without any specific guidelines. When the participants were asked to recall all that they could remember about each story the mindful groups significantly outperformed the other groups. Even though the participants in the mindful groups had more to think about they recalled much more. Thinking back to chapter 2, this would seem to correlate quite well with the idea that quality practice is more beneficial than simple repetition. Whether it is knowing how and what to practice or being encouraged to notice "novelty within the stimulus" (p. 43) when paying attention, the learning will be more effective.

Curiosity

From what I have presented so far (not only in this chapter but in part one of this book) it would appear that learning mindfully is more effective than simple imitation and repetition. The learner is encouraged to discover; to vary their target of attention and notice novelty; to make mistakes and problem solve; to practice with purpose and increase their level of internal awareness; and to rely more on intrinsic feedback. All of this leads to, and encourages, curiosity – a strong desire to know and learn and this, in turn, leads to growth.

While the subject of growth will be examined more thoroughly in part four of this book it is worth highlighting, at this point, that Scott Barry Kaufmann (2020) talks about growth being underpinned by love, purpose and exploration. Curiosity is at the heart of exploration; consequently, it would follow that if during the process of learning you are encouraged to be curious you will, in turn, experience growth as you learn. So, within the LEFG coaching method the way that you learn is foundational to everything else that follows.

> Curiosity is at the heart of exploration which, in turn, promotes 'growth' as you learn.

Skiing curiosity

PART TWO
ENJOY

"I want to be what I was when I wanted to be what I am now".
Graffiti, London, 1980

CHAPTER 5

Develop and nurture your passion

> Questions to ponder:
>
> ⇒ What is passion?
> ⇒ Should you always be enjoying what you do?
> ⇒ How do passion and motivation work together?

The previous section of this book has been all about learning; from finding those initial interests and then developing the necessary skills in order to acquire, at least, a degree of competency. Whether or not you decide to pursue an interest all the way to mastery is a decision that you will make along the way, and as I remarked at the end of chapter 2, your goal may simply be to become accomplished in your chosen activity and to gain enjoyment from it and there is nothing wrong with that.

But it is your longer-term goals and dreams that are a foundation for passion, and it is passion that will provide the emotional fuel for maintaining your interests and driving you forward towards your goals.

86 DEVELOP AND NURTURE YOUR PASSION

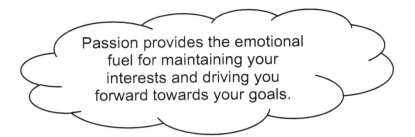

Passion provides the emotional fuel for maintaining your interests and driving you forward towards your goals.

Angela Duckworth, whom I mentioned in chapter 1 when talking about the psychology of interest, is a professor of psychology at the University of Pennsylvania, working alongside Martin Seligman on the MAPP programme (the first University to offer the positive psychology master's degree). I was fortunate to listen to her 'live' at the Fifth World Congress on Positive Psychology in Montreal in July 2017. Duckworth is well known for her construct of 'grit' which she defines as "perseverance and passion towards long-term goals" (Duckworth, Peterson, Matthews, & Kelly, 2007, p. 1087). So, passion is one of the two components that make up grit and combine to work towards your long-term goals. But what exactly is passion?

Duckworth (2016) says that passion is often associated with "intense emotions" (p. 57) and "sustained, enduring devotion" (p. 58). For me, I would say that my real passion is 'living in the alps' and that skiing, and teaching the sport, provided the vehicle to allow me to realise my passion day in day out. I can quite honestly say that every time I go hiking or skiing in the alps, I experience intense positive emotions such as awe, joy, gratitude and serenity and that generates sustained and enduring devotion to do the things that I need to do in order to 'be' in this beautiful environment. Therefore, it is passion that creates the *motivation* to do all the things necessary to make your dreams a reality and it is motivation that drives you forward and creates action.

Human motivation

Motivation moves you towards your goals; short, medium and long-term. Passion, as I have described it above, is often something that develops over time and links to the bigger picture i.e., longer-term goals e.g., such as living in a particular part of the world. Passion creates motivation and when coupled with success motivation creates momentum, but it is important to realise that motivation is not permanent, so you need to keep filling the mind with the right kind of information. In other words, you need to keep filling and topping up the motivation tank. That way when the inevitable setbacks occur, when working towards your goals, you will be in a better position to *respond* and take the necessary action rather than *react* and lose interest or crumble. Responding is the positive way forward, while reacting is negative (Ziglar, 1997).

In psychology, human motivation is a huge subject that spans across different fields such as humanistic, social, sport and positive psychology. There are many different types of motivation (and labels thereof) but for the purposes of this chapter and the subjects of passion and enjoyment I will look at it under two broad headings; intrinsic and extrinsic. While in one sense this helps to simplify the subject this in no way tries to belittle, or undermine, its complexity and the many factors that affect it, as will be seen from the ensuing discussion.

Intrinsic and extrinsic motivation

Intrinsic motivation comes from within and drives your behaviour because the activity is naturally satisfying to you. Furthermore, it is "the inherent tendency to seek out novelty and challenges, to extend and exercise one's capacities, to explore and to learn" (Ryan & Deci, 2000, p. 70). Interestingly this definition links beautifully to what has already been discussed in the chapters on learning and in particular relates to aspects of mindful learning such as novelty and exploration. Therefore, it would be easy to conclude that intrinsic motivation is the best source of motivation? But is that being a little too hasty? Read on and all will be revealed.

Richard Ryan and Edward Deci (2000) are well known for their work on **self-determination theory** (SDT), which is the study of human motivation and personality and one's propensity to grow inherently. SDT posits that **self-motivated** behaviour is driven by three universal psychological needs; *competence*, *autotomy* and *social connection*. SDT is all about the individual having choice and control over the activities that they do, which plays an important role in overall mental health and well-being. Thus, it hugely impacts motivation, as those who feel they have control over the outcome are more likely to take action. Intrinsic motivation plays an important role in self-determined behaviour as can be seen from the earlier definition from Ryan and Deci.

In sport **self-motivation** (the ability to keep doing what needs to be done) is imperative for maintaining interest, continuing to practice and improving performance. James Loehr (1986) suggests that athletes lose motivation when their needs for *recognition*, *approval* and *self-worth* are threatened. In other words when a competitive athlete feels that a lack of success, or losing, undermines the aforementioned, motivation will be lost. Intrinsic motivation is, therefore, not quite the same as self-motivation, because intrinsic motivation is about doing the activity for its own sake, where "the activity itself is the reward" (Csikszentmihalyi, Latter & Duranso, 2017 p. 49). Whereas self-motivation (which can be wholly intrinsic) also includes internally driven behaviour towards an extrinsic outcome/reward. This means that the self-motivated individual has some choice and a degree of control over the process.

Extrinsic motivation is where behaviour is driven by *external rewards* such as money, status, praise, attaining qualifications etc. Of course, rather more negatively, behaviour can also be driven by *punishment* such as the threat of losing one's job, or not wanting to fail. Ryan and Deci (2000) define it as "the performance of an activity to attain some separable outcome" (p. 71). External rewards can vary hugely but there is little doubt, amongst theorists, that "rewards can be used as a technique of control" (Deci, Koestner & Ryan, 1999, p. 657) over people's behaviour. SDT, as mentioned earlier, is about individual choice and control over outcomes, hence extrinsic motivation can vary greatly in this regard form having, to not having, such control.

Passion, motivation and long-term goals
So, what type of motivation is best, or indeed healthier, for developing and nurturing your passion and making progress towards longer-term goals? Or is such a question too simplistic? As alluded to earlier, it is passion

that creates motivation, but there would seem to be a chicken and egg scenario here, because if passion creates motivation then how can motivation develop and nurture passion? Feasibly the answer lies in the idea that it is more cyclical; passion creates motivation, which in turn enhances passion, which builds more motivation and so on. Remember, also, that passion relates to your long-term goals and dreams and therefore, will create motivation to do *whatever things are required* in order to realise those dreams, even if some of the activities themselves are not intrinsically rewarding but more of a means to an end. That would suggest that some activities, if being done as a means to realising bigger life goals, may not be done because they are inherently satisfying (or even enjoyable). And this leads back to SDT and Deci and Ryan's (1985) sub theory 'organismic integration theory' (OIT), which suggests there are different forms of extrinsic motivation which are governed by the amount of choice, or lack thereof, that a person has when engaging in an activity. Conceivably, also, when engaging in said activity there will be more than one reason (motivation) for doing so? Let me explain my thinking here by looking at my own motivations for writing this book, and in so doing expand on Deci and Ryan's OIT.

When I was out on one of my hikes in the mountains (a great place for thinking), I asked myself the question, "why am I writing this book?" Apart from the obvious answer of it being something to do during coronavirus lockdown I came up with seven different reasons;

1) I very much enjoy writing and have become aware over the last three years in particular that it is one of my realised strengths (Linley & Bateman, 2018).

2) I enjoy the mental challenge that writing provides and the required background study, understanding of concepts and resolving of perceived conflicts in different theories.
3) To create a piece of work that will help others with their lives by sharing my life experiences.
4) To make use of all the knowledge that I have accrued particularly during the MAPP course, but also from my life of teaching and learning, and to share that with others.
5) To create something that I am proud of and that will be part of my legacy and contribution to learning, teaching and psychology.
6) To gain praise from others and recognition as an author.
7) To gain monetary reward from book sales.

The OIT is presented as a continuum with nonself-determined behaviour at one end, and completely 'self-determined' at the other. Amotivation is an unwillingness to act, or take action without intent, hence is the ultimate of nonself-determined behaviour. Extrinsic motivation is then sub divided into four categories; moving from very externally driven behaviour and lack of choice, to internally driven behaviour where there is more choice but still some "separable outcome" (Ryan & Deci, 2000, p. 71). Finally, intrinsic motivation is the ultimate of self-determined behaviour. So, where do my reasons for writing this book fit with the OIT continuum?

Reasons one and two are very much about intrinsic motivation and self-determined behaviour because I am undertaking the project for the sheer personal challenge and enjoyment and the inherent satisfaction.

Reasons three and four involve a result other than pure enjoyment (albeit a laudable one and indeed one which will hopefully give subsequent enjoyment). This is still classified as a form of extrinsic motivation, even though it is very close to intrinsic motivation, because it involves a separable outcome i.e., share with others and is therefore not completely done for inherent enjoyment.

Reason five is about creating something that is important to me. This makes it slightly internal in that the outcome is of personal value and the process internally driven.

Reason six is all about my ego and feelings of self-worth! This makes it slightly external in so far as the goal is to demonstrate ability and is driven by what others think.

Reason seven is the classic from of extrinsic motivation where external reward of money from sales is the outcome. Interestingly, this final reason, which is a very extrinsic from of motivation is driven by the need to do whatever things are required in order to realise my dreams thus relates directly back to my passion of living in the alps and the need to earn a living to maintain that goal.

So, it would appear that the motivations to do something can be many and that oftentimes they will be a mixture of intrinsic and extrinsic reasons. My example spans the whole continuum of the OIT (with the exception of amotivation), but it is still more heavily weighted towards the self-determined end of the spectrum. Thus, the answer to the questions posed about which form of motivation is best is, indeed, not simple and is complicated by whether the activity is being done purely for the activity's sake, or whether it is part of the bigger picture and your passion for longer-term goals. However, I would suggest that whenever possible that activities should be more internally driven than externally driven as this is more likely to lead to "sustained, enduring devotion" (Duckworth, 2016, p. 58).

Before introducing several exemplars of passion and in summary of the discussion so far Figure 7 illustrates how passion, motivation and long-term goals interact with each other.

94 DEVELOP AND NURTURE YOUR PASSION

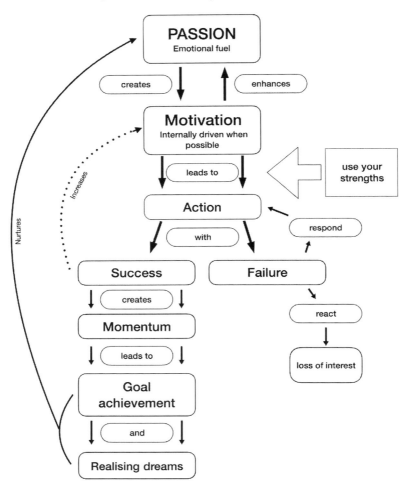

Figure 7.

Exemplars of passion

One of the best ways to understand how you might develop and nurture your own passion is by hearing other people's stories. As you read these stories keep in mind the preceding discussion and ask yourself how these people's stories relate to passion, motivation and long-term goal achievement.

Chamonix Mont Blanc provides the perfect venue for a whole host of sports, both summer and winter, and is the perfect place to develop and nurture your passions. It is the trail running capital of the world hosting the famous Ultra Trail du Mont Blanc (UTMB)[15]. It is also a very famous climbing destination with some of the world's most iconic peaks a must for any serious climber. Hiking (including the famous Tour du Mont Blanc) and mountain biking are also incredibly popular. Then there are the more extreme sports such as paragliding, wingsuit flying, highlining etc., and then, of course, you have the winter sports of skiing, snowboarding, ski touring, ice climbing, snow shoeing etc.

With all this in mind meet Dee O'Neill; trail runner, ski instructor and ski tourer. Dee lives for her time in the mountains whether it is in Chamonix or back home in Ireland in the Wicklow mountains. Here is what Dee says about her mountain passions:

> "I've two major passions in life running and skiing. I could talk for hours on end about both, lose hours

---

[15] The UTMB comprises of a number of trail running races the most famous of which is the UTMB itself a 170km race around Mont Blanc passing through France, Italy and Switzerland.
https://utmbmontblanc.com/en/home

scouting out new routes on maps. Discuss route choices and conditions with friends. Mountains, for me, are addictive, they are a place of adventure and uncertainty making their own everchanging rules. They draw you in and never let go. I'm drawn to the uncertainty, the sudden changing of plans and routes. Getting stuck out for a lot longer than planned because you found a new trail and couldn't resist the temptation to explore. Running out of supplies, it's all part of the adventure. Coping with these sudden changes will have a major impact on how you interpret your adventure. For me it's a new learning experience which can either be positive or negative. Turning the negative experience into a positive learning experience is difficult especially when things have really gone wrong. These are the days where you learn the most and take them into the next adventure!

The mountains make me feel free, free from everything, every stressful thought just disappears. Running can have that effect, you feel pain, you accept it, you accept that your journey is going to be hard. You can feel incredibly awful and then feel on top of the world. Smile on the outside even though you may be dying on the inside, this is something that I take through all my adventures. Smile and the mountains will smile back. There has never been a day that has gone by that I've regretted being in the mountains. Mountains are an addiction that never let go and I never want them to let go".

What is so striking about Dee's description is that trail running, and skiing are simply the means for getting out into the mountains (her true passion) and challenging herself, and those challenges are tough providing a range of emotions (positive and negative), leading to ups and downs and learning from things that go wrong. This links beautifully to the earlier model (Figure 7.) showing that action can lead to success and/or failure, but the important thing is to 'respond' to those so-called failures and learn from them and take that into the next adventure and Dee has indeed had many adventures. In addition to being a highly qualified ski instructor and very experienced ski tourer her list of trail running competitions is very impressive and includes the UTMB races; OCC, CCC, TDS and other alpine trail races including the Marathon du Mont Blanc, Grand Trail Courmayeur, High Trail Vanoise and Irish based races; Mourne Mountain Skyline and Wicklow Way 50.

But you don't have to be a trail runner or skier to live in the Chamonix region and nurture your passion. Meet Kirst Galley who lives in Saint Gervais les Bains in the heart of the Chamonix Mont Blanc region. Kirst, born and raised in Sydney, Australia grew up hiking in the bush and riding horses. Looking for a 'sea change' she decided to move the family to the European Alps. I asked Kirst to describe her passion for the mountains and outdoor life and this is what she said:

> "My passion for the mountains comes from my Dad who loved the outdoors and taught me from an early age to have a love affair with hiking. I love what you experience when you hike, the peacefulness of being in the mountains, the animals you see, marmots are a highlight every

year, and how your senses come alive. For me, climbing Mont Blanc is the ultimate challenge, I look at it every day and would love the satisfaction of knowing I had conquered it. The joy of learning new climbing skills and techniques and competing with myself to be the fittest I can be and to push myself out of my comfort zone are all quite big for someone who had never seen snow till they moved to the alps. After I conquer Mont Blanc learning to ski and then ski touring will be amongst my next challenges. I am lucky enough to live in a place where I can enjoy my passions while always learning something new and pushing myself".

Kirst's description beautifully sums up what I have covered thus far with the LEFG method; talking about **learning** new skills and pushing herself out of her comfort zone and into the stretch zone, while having clear goals and challenges that she wants to achieve and she clearly gets a great deal of **enjoyment** as she pursues these challenges in such a beautiful environment. At the time of writing this Kirst successfully completed her ascent of Mont Blanc along with her friend Jane Williams and mountain guide Bruce Goodlad[16].

While Chamonix Mont Blanc offers a perfect venue for developing and nurturing your passions relating to sport and outdoor life, (living here, of course, makes me slightly biased), what is just as important is that you create the

---

[16] There is a good deal of preparation and acclimatisation required for climbing Mont Blanc. For more information and to grasp Kirst's achievement go to:
http://mountainadventurecompany.com/alpine/mont-blanc/

DEVELOP AND NURTURE YOUR PASSION

opportunities and go to the great places that fire up your enthusiasm. With that in mind meet Sharon Crossan. This is what Sharon had to say when I asked her about her life in sport:

> "Sport is what my life revolves around - research, participating, competing, teaching, instructing, learning, managing, the list is endless. I often wonder how this passion developed, and consider it came from loving the physical and mental challenge, and the determination, attitude and drive to develop myself holistically. What started with a dedication to football and hockey as a child, turned into a love of many sports, and in adulthood has become a life changing dedication to my work and personal life. Representing Scotland in junior hockey, travelling the world as a ski instructor gaining qualifications and learning to become the best ski teacher I could be. Now playing international masters hockey for Scotland in countries I never ski in, or pushing myself to physical limits on skis, the pitch, or running, swimming, or on a bike competing in triathlon and ironman events. Passion is a strong inclination towards an activity that I love, where I invest time and energy and it defines my identity. When you love what you do, what looks like hard work to others is simply an enjoyable activity.
>
> When sport is your life, it is often difficult to determine what is work and what is personal life. With a passion for sport, this is less important, as they blend together. After many years of dedicating my life to participating and competing

in sport, gaining high level coaching and instructing qualifications in many sports, and sharing my love and passion with others, the next progression was following the academic pathway to a Degree in Sports Studies, Physical Education and Professional Education. The teaching of PE and Sport encouraged my passion even more, with new direction and dedication to my learning. Being in the privileged role of a teacher and being involved in developing a love and passion for PE and Sport in children, brings a whole new dimension. I thought learning resilience and mental toughness came naturally in the process. Whether passion can be taught is debatable, but one thing is for sure, the job of teaching may not be easy, but the challenge of it certainly fuels my passion for PE and Sport even more. Passion and purpose allow movement through the tough times. Resilience must be hardwired for me, as my commitment to competing and the long hours to remain fit continues. But dedication, passion and purpose for meeting goals and overcoming obstacles is clearly a way of life, all developed by a simple love of sport".

What is clear from Sharon's writings is that she is incredibly passionate about many sports and has structured her life and created opportunities in order to allow her passion to also be her work. While she may favour some sports over others it seems that her real passion is a life that allows everything to revolve around 'sport'. For her sport is a way of life. Whether the 'activity' itself is your passion, or simply a vehicle towards realising your passion is not really what is important here. Indeed, both the activity and what it leads to may be your

DEVELOP AND NURTURE YOUR PASSION

passions. But what is important is that you develop passion because as I have already discussed it is vital for creating motivation, maintaining interests and driving you forwards. It is the emotional fuel, but it is also personal and all the exemplars of passion, who have contributed to this chapter (including myself), illustrate a great deal of passion for their chosen activities and their goals and dreams.

So, the message is, let your passion develop over time. Understand it by understanding the motivation that is created by it. Know the reasons why you are working towards specific goals and to what extent they are internally and/or externally driven. This will help increase motivation further and lead to the all-important sustained action that is resilient to the inevitable ups and downs that will come along. Then you too can achieve great things.

Trail running

CHAPTER 6

Enjoy the journey

> Questions to ponder:
>
> ⇒ Should you concentrate on the process or the outcome?
> ⇒ How can you 'relax' and enjoy the journey?
> ⇒ Does the 'journey' ever truly end?

In the late 90s I read a book called 'Secrets of super achievers' by Philip Baker (1997) and it contained the quote, at the start of part two of this book, "I want to be what I was when I wanted to be what I am now" (p. 113) and it had a profound impact on me, primarily, because it made me take stock of the *journeys* in my life to that point and look forward to the ones still to come.

My first significant career journey was my progress through the BASI qualification pathway. For me, this was a six-year journey from 1986 to 1992. At that time there were three levels in the British system; Grade 3 Ski Instructor, Grade 2 Ski Teacher and Grade 1 National Ski Teacher. On starting out the idea of attaining the top level was beyond anything that I could imagine. I was just wanting to get my Grade 3. But as is the human way, once I had achieved that level, I wanted to keep going. I remember returning to the Ski Club of Ireland, the artificial ski slope in Dublin where I had my very first lessons before going to Bulgaria with my school, and I was overwhelmed by the adulation and congratulations from my fellow members and instructors. I had joined a very small group of club members who had achieved a BASI qualification. I revelled in my achievement and the sheer excitement of the journey to date.

Fast forward to one year later, buzzing with excitement from another great winter season, I returned to the ski club having passed my Grade 2. Strangely this time the congratulations were more muted. Was it simply expected that I would progress through the system? Or was there a touch of jealously among some members? After all, only two other members had ever achieved that level and they both went on to get the Grade 1.

So, it was no real surprise that when four years later I attained the highest level there did not seem to be much interest at all. Perhaps I had simply outgrown the club where I started? Maybe I was placing too much value on 'external' praise and validation at the expense of fully enjoying the journey? Conceivably I had started to focus too much on the outcome making it all too serious? But the strangest thing of all was that, on achieving the Grade 1, I felt really flat and just a sense of relief. I had become consumed by the goal to the point I just wanted to get it done. Now I'm not saying that I did not enjoy the journey, because I did (albeit more so early on), but the sense of flatness came from the fact that the journey was over. What now? It was the journey that I had enjoyed more than the goal. I wanted to be what I was when I was striving for the goal.

Process vs. outcome

Dr. Jim Taylor is a sports psychologist who has made his name working with alpine ski racers. Dave Burrows (who created and hosts 'The Ski Instructor Podcast'[17]) released an interview with him on 28th February 2020 and one of the things he talked about was the importance of focusing on the process more than the outcome. Coupled with having the right attitude i.e., one that focuses on what you need to do on a day to day basis, or within a specific practice session, it is about controlling what you can control right now, while being aware of, and managing, expectations and not building up the outcome to be something of much greater importance than it warrants. For most people, and situations, the attainment of an outcome goal is not a life and death situation and the result of not achieving it would be disappointment. Perspective is important. So, remember to ask yourself, do I really *need* to achieve this, or would it be nice?

The labels that are used both in wider literature and scientific studies in relation to goals varies considerably. For example, focusing on the process as described above could be equated to learning goals, task goals or mastery goals all of which are seen as relatively interchangeable (Grant & Dweck, 2003). The key point to understand here is that the process is something that you control as part of the journey while the outcome is not something that is directly in your control.

---

[17] The Ski Instructor Podcast episode 16:
https://podcasts.apple.com/gb/podcast/16-dr-jim-taylor-us-ski-team-and-world-cup-psychologist/id1451514234?i=1000466983042

Flexibility of your goals

With the understanding that the outcome is not always in your control being flexible about your goals is another way to help you to relax and enjoy the journey. There is nothing worse than setting a goal and then being so rigidly fixed on the steps you need to take that all the enjoyment simply ebbs away. Expecting the pathway to your outcome goal to go exactly as planned is completely unrealistic given how life tends to unfold. When I train ski instructors for the 'teaching' elements of their exams I always stress that "the only reason you make a lesson plan is so that you have something that can be changed". Furthermore, I highlight that, if they deliver a lesson exactly as they planned then it is highly likely it will be a poor lesson because they will have invariably failed to respond to the individuals within the group and their needs plus the challenges posed by the ever changing environment. Therefore, it is the same when setting goals in life – make a plan so that you have something to change!

Savouring the joys of the journey

Living your life in the present, at least for a good proportion of the time, is vital, not only for enjoying the journey but also for full engagement in whatever you are doing. The latter will be covered in great detail in part three of this book when I delve into *flow* sharing more about the research I and many others have done. Mindfulness is also very important for being present and this has already been covered in chapter 4 and will be revisited in a number of the chapters still to come. However, another very effective technique for remaining present, and for enhancing the present, is *savouring*.

In simple terms savouring means appreciating the things that are happening right now. Savouring is very much a part of positive psychology and an important aspect of people's overall well-being. Fred Bryant and Joseph Veroff (1984) looked at dimensions of subjective mental health and concluded that self-assessing one's ability to enjoy positive experiences was a missing aspect of psychological well-being. This led them to assert that savouring was what was missing, which they define as having the capacities "to attend to, appreciate, and enhance" positive experiences that occur in people's lives (Bryant & Veroff, 2012, p. 2).

Sonja Lyubomirsky (2010) says that savouring differs slightly from flow in that, "savouring requires a stepping outside of experience and reviewing it, whereas flow involves a complete immersion in the experience" (p. 197).

She also mentions that you can savour in different ways;

- **in the present** – by noticing and being aware of what is happening and appreciating the good things, whether that is listening to your favourite music, walking in the mountains and admiring a stunning view, enjoying good company with friends etc.;
- **in the past** – by remembering good events and moments from your life such as a great holiday, successes you had when learning a new skill or other achievements;
- **in the future** – by looking forward and imagining successful future events.

And while savouring the past and the future take you away from the present they can serve as ways of enhancing the present through stimulating positive emotions such as gratitude, pride, inspiration and hope.

Finding enjoyment even in adversity

For most people enjoying the journey and living life in the present simply means coping with the relatively normal ups and downs of life and learning the skills of savouring, mindfulness and flow. While for others life can sometimes deal them a very challenging hand!

David Smith MBE is someone who was dealt such a hand and his story is truly inspiring and a lesson to everyone about making the most of their lives.

David comes from Aviemore in the Spey Valley of the Scottish Highlands and was born with a defect called clubfoot[18]. Despite having to wear what he described as 'forest gump boots'[19] to correct the defect he fell in love with sport and over the years has competed/participated in; shinty (Scottish Gaelic sport playing for Newtonmore), karate (GB squad for six years), track athletics (becoming East of Scotland 400m champion), bobsleigh (GB team as brakeman) and skiing (working as a British team coach in the days when Alain Baxter, The Highlander, was competing on the World Cup). Then in Paralympic sports; rowing (winning gold at the Paralympics of London 2012 in the mixed cox four) and cycling as part

---

[18] Clubfoot is a birth defect where one or both feet are rotated inward and downward https://en.wikipedia.org/wiki/Clubfoot
[19] David Smith MBE | Fighting Cancer, Paralysis and making Toyko | 2012 Paralympic Champion https://youtu.be/M7CkLk2t320

of team GB. In 2013 he was awarded an MBE in the New Year's Honours list. He says "sport has given me so much"[20] which is certainly true, but apart from the astonishing achievements of competing and being involved in so many sports, at such a high level, having been born with clubfoot, that does not begin to describe why David's story is so inspirational.

In May 2010 a cancerous tumour was discovered in David's spinal cord. That month he had what would be the first of six surgeries (at the time of writing) related to removing the tumour. Soon after being discharged he suffered a hematoma and was rushed back into hospital to have the clot removed. This caused temporary paralysis and he had to learn to walk again from scratch. In spite of this he was back training within months and went on to win gold at the World Rowing Championships in the mixed cox four, at lake Bled in Slovenia, before going on to his London 2012 Paralympic triumph.

But unfortunately for David the tumour would return and in October 2014 he had further surgery. His goal following this surgery was to cycle up Mt. Ventoux in southern France as part of his preparation for the Rio 2016 Olympics[21] (initially the goal was simply to cycle up once but this changed when he found out there were three different routes up and that others had done all three in the one day). From reading his story, and watching the various videos, what comes to the fore is his

---

[20] David Smith: "My ultimate dream is to live":
https://youtu.be/QRNRU6OH_go
[21] The BBC Scotland 'Dead Man Cycling' documentary covers an 18-month period as David has a second surgery to remove his tumour and works towards climbing Mt. Ventoux:
https://vimeo.com/154181061

incredible work ethic in spite of the pain. He shows immense mental and physical resilience, determination and innovation in training methods. The old adage "no pain no gain" might not be one I would usually advocate preferring something more like "no challenge no gain" but in David's case it is certainly the approach he takes into rehab and one that brings immense results.

David achieved his goal of cycling up Mt. Ventoux three times, on each of the routes, in one day, and was progressing well towards making the GB cycling team for Rio 2016, but the tumour returned, and further surgeries were required with subsequent paralysis and tough rehab. What is amazing about David's story is how he keeps on fighting and draws inspiration from all parts of his journey whether that's sporting role models or children dying on the cancer wards who have the most fantastic attitudes.

Apart from all his sporting achievements David loves challenging his mind and learning. He has a sports science degree from the University of Bath and has more recently been studying positive psychology. He writes a regular column for The Herald, which is not only about his own continuing story but how to deal positively with the COVID-19 pandemic. When I asked him about including his story in this book, he was extremely supportive and encouraging.

It is difficult with just words, and the space afforded in this book, to adequately portray David's story (both past and continuing); therefore, I would highly recommend that you follow the various links in the foot notes and watch the videos. However, one quote from his May 2020 interview[22] nicely sums up so much of what this chapter is all about. David says, "because I think in life we're so focused with goals, we're so focused with trying to achieve things externally, that sometimes we forget about the internal journey and that's really where you find true happiness". And this is so true, if you are to truly enjoy the journey then you need to engage with your feelings and emotions along the way. Emotions (whether perceived as positive or negative) are an integral part of positive psychology (Fredrickson, 2001; Kashdan & Biswas-Diener, 2015; Lomas, 2016; Seligman, 2003) and by connecting with your emotions you can better deal with the challenges of life.

Harnessing additional benefits

Whatever your circumstances, it is the journey that allows you to gain experience, to build your character strengths (Peterson & Seligman, 2004), to develop your interests (see chapter 1), and acquire a whole range of skills. By taking your time to enjoy the experience of the journey, and not just rush towards the outcome goal, many of the benefits you acquire along the way may not have been part of your original plan but will end up being valuable life skills.

In summary

I'll close this chapter with the thought that it is not so much the journey that ends but rather individual voyages in a much greater journey of life. To fully enjoy that journey you should keep embarking on new voyages, which

---

[22] FCE Podcast #6 | David Smith MBE tells his extraordinary story https://youtu.be/XrxpZLGhw7g

involve lifelong learning, while living life in the present through being mindful, seeking flow and savouring the past, present and future. But above all, be grateful for all the joys and emotions you experience as part of your journey and take inspiration from others, like David Smith, who do so in spite of the enormous challenges they face.

> Keep embarking on new voyages, which involve lifelong learning, while living life in the present through being mindful, seeking flow and savouring.

The journey

CHAPTER 7

Perform with creativity

Questions to ponder:

⇒ What is creativity?
⇒ Why should you strive for creativity?
⇒ Can anyone be creative?

As with many of the previous chapters defining some of the key words helps to set the stage for the content that follows, and this is vital for a word like creativity which can mean different things to different people.

Defining creativity

So, what exactly is creativity? And how might it differ in interpretation between different domains? For example, mathematics is a domain, but then so is sport, yet being creative in maths is probably very different to creativity in sport where movement of the body is involved? While being cognizant of other domains such as maths, physics, computing or biochemistry, and how many of the examples and discussions thus far have some relevance and transferability, this book is primarily focused on 'physical movement' and motor skills acquisition be it a sport, or learning a musical instrument, dance, play etc.

In addition, the title of this chapter lends itself to the latter in that it says, 'perform with creativity'.

Therefore, let me begin with a definition of 'creativity' with the caveat that because there are so many definitions available, I have chosen one that I believe *fits* with, and has *relevance* to, this chapter and the book as a whole.

> "Creativity may be defined as ability to produce original ideas and/or actions with flexibility and fluency" (Joffe, n.d.)

First off, the word *ability* suggests that creativity is something that can be learned or at least encouraged, and I will delve into what can help you to become more creative as the chapter unfolds. But at this point the words of Ed Catmull (2014; co-founder of Pixar) seem appropriate, "I believe to my core, that everybody has the potential to be creative – whatever form that creativity takes – and that to encourage such development is a noble thing" (p. xv[23]).

Secondly, the inclusion of the word *actions* in the definition relates to physical movements that are made based on decision-making, which is a mental process. This is highly relevant to the domain of sport where often such decisions would be classed as tactics (the ability to use *flexibility* to apply techniques in a variety of ways based on the external environmental demands). And these tactical decisions need to be executed in a timely manner with *fluency*.

---

[23] Roman numeral – there are several occasions in the book where the page numbers of quotes are Roman numerals.

Performing with creativity

But why should you aspire, or strive, to perform with creativity? Csikszentmihalyi (1997a) helps answer this question when he says, "creative persons find joy in a job well done. Learning for its own sake is rewarding" (p. 5). And it is my assertion that 'performing with creativity' not only enhances learning, but also leads to the emotions of *joy* and *inspiration* during the activity, while after the activity *pride* for a job well done, an increase in *interest* for the activity, as well as an overall feeling of enjoyment are all by-products. Therefore, performing with creativity is an integral feature of the 'ENJOY' part of the LEFG method and by doing so you can increase your own positivity through fostering several of the 10 positive emotions identified by Barbara Fredrickson (2010). And it is posited that people who experience positive emotions on a regular basis are likely to develop greater well-being (Fredrickson, 2001).

Having established, at least to some extent, what creativity means in relation to movement and sport, and why performing with creativity is important in the context of enjoyment, I want to further unpack what it actually means to *perform* with creativity. To aid this process, I decided to ask a number of friends/colleagues the question; what does perform with creativity mean to you? All of these people are skiers or ski instructors, BUT (and of crucial importance for this topic) they all have other very fascinating professions and/or pastimes making their input very valuable to this debate. What was also important, from my perspective, was that I remain completely 'open' to how they each interpret the question. So, let me introduce you to each of them and share their thoughts and then briefly discuss how this adds to what I have already presented;

First up is Helen Trayfoot-Waugh who works as a ski teacher in Châtel, in the Portes du Soleil, in France. Helen skied from the age of four starting out in Austria with an instructor who only spoke German. When her Mum asked her if this bothered her that he didn't speak English she said, "no, it's like dancing, I just copy". Helen balanced skiing with schoolwork, dance, art and music and then on finishing school went to university to do a degree in performing arts and a postgraduate in art constructed textiles. She was drawn back to skiing where she gravitated towards like-minded people who were creative in their lives as well as their skiing, which she initially found in Vermont, USA. In answer to my question about what it means to perform with creativity Helen describes skiing as follows:

> "Yes, there is the thrill of speed and competition and technical elements but for me it is all about the feeling. It is about the sensations I get from moving smoothly and freely – like a dance or playing my cello where the bow must flow in constant curves telling the story through the sound it creates. In skiing I am pressing and balancing through the curves, using the terrain to push me into different directions. It is about stripping it back to its pure essence and smiling as I move to match the curve, the terrain, the mountain".

Next up is Robbie Fenlon who is a mindfulness trainer, Integral coach[24] and IFMGA mountain guide[25]. Robbie was a member of the first Irish Everest expedition in 1993 and has extensive experience guiding trekking tours in Nepal. From 2006 Robbie and I worked together in Chamonix delivering back country skiing courses and developing the mountain safety courses for the Irish Association of Snowsports Instructors. Robbie was also a contributing writer for my first book Parallel Dreams Alpine Skiing (Tate, 2007). Here is what Robbie had to say in response to my question:

> "I think of it more as 'living with creativity'. I have to realise the future is an open canvas. It has never happened before. That calls me/us to meet the present as new and ripe with potential. I/we have to be awake to everything in ourselves and in the world as it is, right now. That way we can live with creativity, free of old beliefs as patterns that lock us in the past. It means anything I/we do is an opportunity for creativity. Even if it is just making a cup of coffee".

Shona Tate began skiing at the age of two! Encouraged by her parents and brother she spent weekends during the winter skiing and racing at Cairngorm, Aviemore, Scotland. She progressed to the Scottish Alpine Ski Team and eventually moved into coaching and teaching the sport. Alongside her skiing she was heavily involved with the Girl Guide Association and this would eventually

---

[24] Integral coaching is based on Ken Wilber's AQAL Integral Theory https://en.wikipedia.org/wiki/Ken_Wilber
[25] IFMGA stands for International Federation of Mountain Guide Associations https://en.wikipedia.org/wiki/UIAGM

take her on to two trips to Ghana, the second of which she co-led, where the team were involved with community building projects. Shona currently runs British Alpine Ski School in Chamonix, France. Her response to the same question was as follows:

> "Referring to perform as a 'doing' or 'delivery' – perform with creativity is taking the receiver on a journey from A to B, that is put across in a way that is inspirational and engaging, not just text book black and white do and don'ts, but included within it is a bit of personality and a lot skill from said performer. It has a uniqueness to it that only that individual can add, which softens the journey to reaching the end goal. The creativity within it is not something that can be taught but instead is created and comes from within the individual. I think of a real true group of Jazz musicians where each musician takes his/her turn to lead the performance, it just happens smoothly and seamlessly, and it is not scripted or written down".

Nancy Chambers has spent her life working and playing in the outdoors. She is passionate about all the sports she does. She is one of the few women to gain the following higher-level outdoor qualifications; WMCI,[26] IML,[27] Level 5 Canoe coach, Senior Sailing Instructor and a number of others at a lower level, including BASI Level 2 Ski Instructor. In addition to these outdoor qualifications Nancy is also a children's author specialising in adventures in the outdoors, a guidebook

---

[26] WMCI stands for Winter Mountaineering and Climbing Instructor.
[27] IML stands for the International Mountain Leader qualification. https://baiml.org/baiml/how-to-become-an-iml/

writer and photographer. Her reply to my question came in two parts with the first being how she observes creativity in others:

> "The best climbers, paddlers etc. to watch are not just the ones that are technically brilliant, but the ones that read their environment and create art out of the movement that they perform whilst travelling through".

She then clarifies why creativity is needed in outdoor sports:

> "In the outdoors we require creativity to visualise and link the skills that we need to navigate safely down a rapid, climb eloquently up a cliff face or inspire others to love our environments".

The final person I asked about what it means to perform with creativity was Tania Cotton who is a movement analyst, performance coach and film producer. Her background as a physiotherapist and health and performance educator has included speaking at many international conferences on health and wellness. In more recent years Tania has been working with the Swiss Olympic Medical Centre in Geneva working with numerous World Class and Olympic athletes alongside some of the world's leading experts in movement, nutrition, athletic development and behavioural change. She is the founder of MovementWise[28] and also hosts the LifeWise[29] podcast. Before answering the question

---

[28] MovementWise from pain to performance
https://movementwise.org
[29] LifeWise podcasts https://movementwise.org/podcast/

about 'perform with creativity' she clarified how she and her colleagues define 'performance':

> "Performance to us means how you do whatever you need to do, or want to do, in your life in a way that enables you to thrive and not just survive".

And in answer to my question Tania said:

> "True freedom of movement comes when we continually discover new ways to connect with ourselves, others and the world around us in ways that enhance our health, happiness and quality of life. To perform with creativity is to explore, discover and push open the boundaries of your ability to express yourself physically, mentally and emotionally. We are as limited as we are inflexible, and lack of self-expression leads to depression".

All of the answers are extremely interesting and, while in one sense, quite varied, in many ways they relate to each other. Taken together they provide some valuable insights into what it means to perform with creativity. For example, Helen talks a lot about heightened internal awareness – feelings, sensations, freedom, constant movement, which are all a response to her external environment. It is as if her actions and awareness merge (see chapter 9 for more on this). Peter Joffe (n.d.) interprets creativity in sport as being decision-making with working memory (WM) being an important part of that process. Working memory is your short-term memory and is concerned with immediate conscious processing. WM is made up of what you feel (intrinsic) hear and see (extrinsic). So, WM allows you to process information quickly, as you are engaged in the activity, through monitoring performance as it happens and making adjustments along the way (see also 'Unambiguous feedback' chapter 8). In skiing, these adjustments come in response to the external environment e.g., snow texture, terrain changes etc., which seems to align to Helen's thoughts.

Robbie is very much concerned with being present moment focused and seizing every opportunity as it presents itself. While on one level he seems to be talking about how you live your life, it is clear that by living life in this way it increases your ability to be creative in the moment, when engaged in a specific task, whatever that might be. It is interesting that Helen talked about gravitating towards like-minded people who were creative in the way they lived their lives. So, feasibly, those who are more inclined to perform with creativity approach their wider lives in this way and associating with others of similar views is a part of that.

Shona talks about both the performer and the teacher with the latter needing to employ strategies that engage the learner, and this would fit with using teaching styles beyond the discovery threshold (Mosston & Ashworth, 2002). The performer needs to be highly skilled (which can also be inferred from Helen's descriptions) and this would suggest that there is a link between expertise and being able to perform with creativity. She also uses the word *uniqueness,* which indicates originality on the part of the performer and this ties in with the original definition by Joffe (n.d.) near the beginning of this chapter. Finally, she talks about the creativity coming from within and that it is not something that is taught. But perhaps it is not creativity itself that is taught/learned but rather other additional skills that promote creativity?

Nancy, like Helen, talks about the link between movements of the body and responding to the external environment. Using the word 'art' in relation to those movements correlates with Shona's suggestion that each performer/performance has uniqueness and hence creativity. Her reference to 'using skills' to cope with these challenging environments while being eloquent infers (like Helen and Shona) that the performer is of a high-level and has expertise. Finally, Nancy (like Shona) mentions using creative performance to inspire others which is a vital role of the teacher to ensure that students are engaged, remain interested and fall in love with both the activity and environment.

Tania very much links performing with creativity with freedom of movement leading to better health and well-being that encompasses the physical, mental and emotional aspects (whole being). This is very much echoed by Kelly McGonigal (2019) throughout her excellent book 'The Joy of Movement' and summed up where she says, "it is as if what is good in us is most easily activated by or accessed through movement" (p. 213).

The 'freedom of movement' that Tania highlights it would seem is a result of being *allowed* to be creative and to respond to what is **within us** (Shona's reference to coming from within the individual), **between us** (with others) and **around us** (the external environment that Helen talked about). And it corelates beautifully with Nancy's description that movement is like *art* that is created while passing through. Finally, Tania warns that not being allowed to express oneself and be creative can lead to depression.

But how do you get to this point of being able to perform with creativity as so eloquently described by Helen, Robbie, Shona, Nancy and Tania? Read on...

Improving your ability to perform with creativity

I introduced the Diamond Model of Skill Acquisition (DMSA) in chapter 2 in the context of practicing with purpose. The advantage of the DMSA is that it combines motor learning with mindful learning and flow theory, and it is this *integration* that facilitates the development of not just motor skills but also encourages the learner to *be* more creative as they learn, and to *perform* with creativity as they become more skilful.

It is during the 'movements' stage of the DMSA, when motor learning is taking place, that the learner can also develop a whole range of additional skills that are the seeds of creativity, as long as a mindful learning approach is adopted. Some of these have been previously mentioned but include; a heightened sense of internal awareness, intrinsic feedback, kinaesthetic awareness, proprioception etc. However, what is of paramount importance is the development of attention skills. This is, of course, part of mindful learning e.g., varied target of attention (chapter 4) and focusing your attention (chapter 3) but additionally, Daniel Memmert (2011) says that "attention is associated with creativity" (p. 94) and that it is specifically the *breadth of attention* that is important e.g., the "number and range of stimuli that a person is able to attend to at any one time" (p. 94). This would seem to be closely related with divided attention (Moran, 1996) mentioned at the outset of chapter 3, and the ability to divide attentional resources between internal and external focuses at the same time (see BEE Focused also chapter 3).

What is, perhaps, unfolding from this discussion, so far, is that the movements stage of the DMSA is a very busy mental period and that learning can be messy and untidy, but that is also what can make it fun and encourage creativity. Discovery, experimenting, imaginative play, making and correcting mistakes should all be happening at this stage. The challenge, for both the learner and the teacher, is recognising this and accepting that 'untidy' and 'messy', at this point in the process, is OK!

During the performance stage of the DMSA the learner will continue to enhance their motor skills and make them more robust. The model specifically highlights that, at this stage, expansion and *creating* variation is the primary concern, referring to how the skills are used and applied. This requires the learner to develop their decision-making skills (which, if you recall, Joffe interprets as creativity in sport) and tactics, which I defined as the ability to use *flexibility* to apply techniques in a variety of ways based on the external environmental demands. This is also one of the most exciting and enjoyable parts of skill acquisition and one of the reasons Helen spoke about smiling as she performs. There would appear to be a link between higher skilled performers (as alluded to by Shona and Nancy), better attentional skills and the ability to perform with creativity, which is supported by research carried out by Daniel Memmert (2011).

Therefore, to reiterate, creativity is encouraged alongside the learning of motor skills during the movements stage of the DMSA and this, in turn, allows the learner to develop their ability to perform with creativity during the performance stage of the DMSA.

A couple of thoughts;

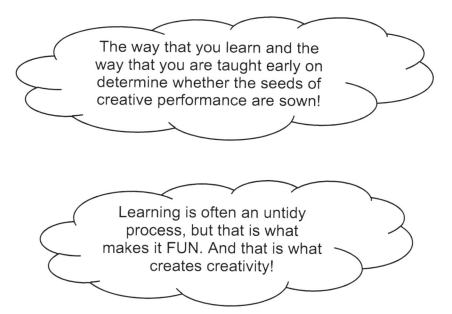

This chapter has clarified what creativity is in relation to motor learning and movement whether that is in sport, dance, music, play etc. It has provided great insights into what it means to perform with creativity in these contexts as well as more widely in life.

The underlying narrative of this book has been that you can become more skilful through learning in the right way, and through practicing with purpose, whether that is a motor skill, a purely mental skill, or something like becoming more creative. But, above all, these processes should be enjoyable and being encouraged to be creative is one of the best routes to ENJOY. Scott Barry Kaufmann and Carolyn Gregoire (2016) say, "we are all in some way wired to create" (p. xxx) so you just need to harness that power whilst recognising that it is not creativity per se that is learnt, but rather all the things that encourage it. Just like happiness, creativity can be elusive if you try to force it. As Shona said creativity is something that "comes from within the individual".

Interestingly creativity and flow are "closely intertwined" (Cseh, 2016, p. 79) as flow helps to drive creativity, while creativity, arguably, generates human progress and achievement. So, it is fitting, and timely, that the third section of this book is all about flow.

The performing arts: Tango in Buenos Aires

PART THREE
FLOW

"Control of consciousness determines the quality of life."

Mihaly Csikszentmihalyi

CHAPTER 8

Foundations are vital

Questions to ponder:

⇒ What exactly is flow?
⇒ Bored, challenged or scared?
⇒ Why is feedback so important?

Flow is a mental state and is also known as 'optimal experience'. It occurs when a person is fully immersed in an activity that is challenging. People who experience flow will have clear goals, gain immediate feedback and perceive the challenge as being very slightly greater than their available skills. The experience itself is rewarding and leads to feelings of enjoyment and satisfaction (Csikszentmihalyi, 1975, 1990, 1993, 1997b).

Most literature refers to flow as having nine dimensions, or components, with the 'labels' varying slightly from one text to another. Figure 8 (Tate, 2018b) illustrates these dimensions with three forming the flow foundations (discussed in the present chapter) and six being flow state characteristics (discussed in chapter 9).

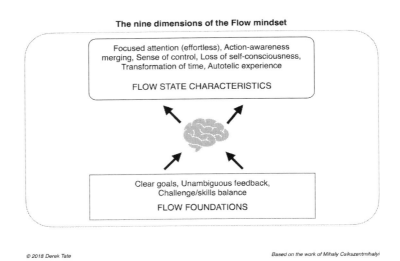

Figure 8.

As will be revealed, in chapter 10, my own research findings led to the proposal of a new model with the dimensions expanding to 10 (Tate, 2019d).

A little history

In psychology flow has been studied since the 1970s. Mihaly Csikszentmihalyi is considered the father of flow and credited with coining the phrase for this psychological construct.

Csikszentmihalyi is a Hungarian-American psychologist although he was born in Rijeka, Croatia (then Fiume in the Kingdom of Italy). In his teenage years he was influenced by the work of famous Swiss psychiatrist Carl Jung who was writing and speaking about the more positive aspects of human experience. This led to him studying psychology and working on aspects such as happiness, creativity and flow. Over the years he has been involved in researching flow and its dimensions with many published articles, books and book chapters to his name.

Much of the flow research since the 1970s has involved subjective self-reports from people's experiences through qualitative interviewing methods. However, methods such as ESM[30] (experiencing sampling method) and questionnaires (about flow state and disposition) have also been used to collect quantitative data. More recently fMRI (brain-imaging) has offered some exciting measurement possibilities (see Ulrich, Keller, & Gro, 2016).

Flow has also been studied in many different settings including the workplace and with various leisure activities. Susan Jackson (Jackson, 1992; Jackson & Csikszentmihalyi, 1999; Jackson & Eklund, 2002) was one of the first to research flow in sport and since then there have been a host of other people including most notably Christian Swann (Swann, 2016; Swann, Crust, Keegan, Piggott, & Hemmings, 2015).

As a subject flow is frequently written about and authors such as Steven Kotler (2015), George Mumford (2016)

---

[30] The Experience Sampling Method is, in effect, a daily diary for recording thoughts about activities at stages throughout the day and was developed by Mihaly Csikszentmihalyi and Reed Larson. More info is available in Csikszentmihalyi's collected works (2014) – see chapter references.

and Amy Saltzman (2018) are amongst those who have popularised the topic.

Closer to home (for me anyway) The European Flow Researchers Network[31] (EFRN) comprises of many leading academics who aim to develop a more common understanding and measurement of the construct.

Mental and physical?

At the outset of this chapter I referred to flow as a mental state. However, the context of this book is about the combination of physical movement and psychological processes e.g., motor learning in skill acquisition. So, being in flow during a physical activity means that there is a synergy between mind and body. Top sports performers like Roger Federer are the epitome of mind and body working in harmony and there is little doubt that Federer will regularly experience flow state. Physical activities that have clear goals, rules and challenge requisite skills (e.g., organised sports) are the ideal route to experiencing flow (Csikszentmihalyi, 2002).

But while flow experiences can often lead to *peak performance*, that is not always the case and they are not one in the same (in spite of what some literature and websites might portray!). Indeed, an athlete may achieve peak performance and not enter a flow state a view supported by Richard Cox (1998). Furthermore, Cox

---

[31] The EFRN website is https://efrn.webs.com/ and their stated mission is to develop and share a common understanding of the concept and measurement of flow based on rigorous scientific standards.

says when referring to flow state that, "it is sometimes, but not necessarily, associated with peak performance" (p. 122).

Having now established what flow is, and its origins, I will look at the three foundations in turn; clear goals, unambiguous feedback and challenge skills balance.

F1: Clear goals

The setting of goals has been covered earlier in this book in relation to overall practice session goals (chapter 2) and longer-term goals (chapter 5). In this section the focus will be on setting clear task specific goals.

Setting task goals either for a practice session or an event, such as a competition, not only directs action but also provides clarity of what needs to be done. In other words, the objective(s) is/are clear. I deliberately included the plural as each task may have more than one objective. In addition, it should be noted that the duration of the task may vary considerably. For example, the men's cycling road race at the Rio Olympics 2016 was won in a time of 6:10:05 by Greg Van Avermaet of Belgium whereas Mikaela Shiffrin won the alpine skiing Super-G race in Bansko, Bulgaria in January 2020 in a time of 1:10.88. Consequently, the number and type of goals that are set for an event that lasts just over a minute will be very different to one that lasts several hours. In addition, a cycling road race (unless it's a time trail) will involve goals that relate to competitors' position as the race unfolds, whereas the majority of alpine skiing races are individual events against the clock. Another consideration here is that entering and maintaining flow state for long periods of time is unlikely so in the cycling example a competitor may only experience flow for certain periods of the race.

In my own environment of teaching skiing the tasks that I set my learners will typically last for just a matter of seconds as we progress down sections of the ski run (piste). Typically, the same task may be repeated several times but what is crucial is that the learner is crystal clear about the objective of the task and what outcome they are trying to achieve. Whether I am working with children or adults having some kind of objective is important and when I use drills to develop skills, I want my learners to understand how the drill is improving the skill i.e., what is the purpose of the drill?

Setting clear goals for each task is not only important from the point of view of increasing the likelihood of entering a flow state, but it also means that deriving feedback is much easier as there is something to measure the performance against which leads nicely onto the second foundation.

F2: Unambiguous feedback

There are a number of feedback sources available to the performer of a physical task (see Lockerbie & Tate, 2012). Feedback can be ongoing, during the task itself, and can come after/before the performance. Feedback can come from an *external source* e.g., coach/teacher, peer, video playback etc., or from *the performer themselves*, as a direct result of moving e.g., kinaesthetic awareness (feelings and sensations of the body's movements), proprioception (the body's ability to know where it is in space), visual or auditory cues (from the immediate environment). In sports, and where physical movement is concerned, feedback from the performer themselves is referred to as 'intrinsic feedback'.

On a point of clarification here; 'intrinsic feedback' is a combination of using an internal and external focus of attention (see BEE Focused chapter 3) with the latter being required to interpret the immediate environment.

Therefore, on-going and immediate feedback (as the task is being executed), from the performer themselves (intrinsic), allows for instant knowledge of progress so that adjustments can be constantly made to meet the current demands of the activity. This is an essential foundational requirement of flow and is called 'unambiguous feedback'.

A good example of the need for unambiguous feedback is the sport of rock climbing. In all forms of climbing this kind of feedback is essential, but it becomes very obvious how vital this is when engaging in solo climbing (with rope backup), or free solo (without rope and where a fall could result in injury or death). The performer is at one with the rock face, or pitch, and knows immediately how well they are doing. Each movement is deliberate and uses all of the aforementioned cues. To get a sense of how important unambiguous feedback is for climbing watch the documentary movie The Dawn Wall[32] about climbers Tommy Caldwell and Kevin Jorgeson's first free ascent of the dawn wall of El Capitan in the Yosemite National Park.

---

[32] The Dawn Wall Documentary film is available on https://www.dawnwall-film.com

One of my primary goals as a ski teacher is to help my learners develop their intrinsic feedback skills. It is not uncommon for students in any sport, or activity, to overly rely on extrinsic feedback especially from the coach or teacher. This not only makes improvement (skill development) less likely, but also *inhibits* rather than facilitates flow. This is where skilful use of teaching styles (Mosston & Ashworth, 2002) can help to develop the learner's ability to redress the need for constant extrinsic feedback. The self-check teaching style, for example, is a great way to improve the learner's kinaesthetic awareness during performance while augmenting the information gained with extrinsic feedback after the performance has been done.

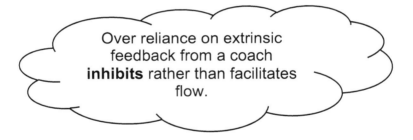

Over reliance on extrinsic feedback from a coach **inhibits** rather than facilitates flow.

In summing up the foundation of 'unambiguous feedback', in the context of physical movement, the words of Mihaly Csikszentmihalyi are appropriate – "the simple act of moving the body across space becomes a source of complex feedback" (2002, p. 95) and when the performer themselves learns to use this immediate feedback, in real time, there is a much greater chance of entering a flow state.

Flow in creativity

Before discussing the third foundation of flow I want to address an apparent 'conflict' with flow in creativity, and specifically the arts, in relation to the foundations of clear goals and unambiguous feedback. Because sports are governed by rules and generally have specific aims, whether measured objectively; through goals/points scored or against the clock, or subjectively; by being judged against a set of criteria (like in ski instructor exams), the setting of goals is fairly straightforward. Not only that, but by knowing what has to be achieved moment-by-moment the participant is more likely to experience flow. Even the musician will know exactly what a piece of music should sound like and know the sequence of notes to play. But what about a music composer/writer? Or an artist painting a picture? The composer will know that he/she wants to write a piece for a particular genre, but otherwise the outcome will be unclear. While the artist may be equally vague about what the finished painting will actually look like.

Genevieve Cseh (2016) argues that most flow research has focused on organised activities, such as sports and playing music, where there are not only clear rules, but where the activities themselves can be practiced and automated. As a result, she questions whether the components of flow are experienced in the same way across all domains especially in the arts? In particular she targets the foundations of clear goals and unambiguous feedback saying that they "have received the least critical attention from researchers" (p. 80). The key difference between the arts and other activities is that creativity in this domain is difficult to define and art is incredibly subjective therefore using feedback to measure progress towards a goal is difficult as there are no clearly defined/accepted criteria. Csikszentmihalyi (2002) describes these activities as being 'open ended' and says that, "in some creative activities, where goals are not clearly set in advance, a person must develop a strong personal sense of what she intends to do" (p. 55). He goes on to suggest that people in these creative activities will have developed an internal sense of what is good and what is bad and stresses that "without such internal guidelines, it is impossible to experience flow" (p. 56).

So, perhaps, the answer lies in the fact that through experience artists are able to measure their own success against their own internalised criteria, developed over time, allowing them to know how they are progressing towards their goal (however vague it might be) hence allowing them to experience flow.

F3: Challenge/skills balance
This is probably one of the most interesting and important aspects affecting whether or not you can enter a flow state.

The 'challenge and skills balance' is all about your subjective perception of the level of challenge that a task provides matched against your available skills. Remember that while this book is weighted towards physical activity and the acquisition of motor skills, the task and required skills can be anything that you enjoy doing, find interesting, and which provides a challenge; be it writing, reading, solving a crossword puzzle, playing chess etc.

When there is too little challenge for your available skills this can lead to boredom. On the other hand, too great a challenge can lead to anxiety and fear. What is important is to find the correct balance where your available skills are stretched just enough to provide a challenge. Susan Jackson and Mihaly Csikszentmihalyi (1999) say that, "to experience flow, it is not enough for challenges to equal skills; both factors need to be extending the person, stretching them to new levels" (p. 16). While in the book 'Running Flow' Csikszentmihalyi, Latter and Duranso, (2017) say, "to experience flow, you need to find a challenge that is within reach but still requires effort to achieve" (p. 21). Csikszentmihalyi (1997b) says that "flow tends to occur when a person's skills are fully involved in overcoming a challenge that is just about manageable" (p. 30).

Each of the three quotes provides greater insight into what is meant by the challenge-skills balance, yet they all vary slightly! The first quote from Jackson and Csikszentmihalyi emphasises that both skills and challenges are stretching the person and that by doing so learning and skill development are enhanced. This ties in well with the Diamond Model of Skill Acquisition, presented in chapter 2, where it is suggested that flow is more likely to occur with people who have a high level of skill (e.g., those that are in the 'performance stage' of the DMSA) and who are then challenged by the task. This is another reason why finding flow is such a good thing; because apart from being enjoyable it actually enriches learning and makes skill acquisition more robust. The second quote from 'Running Flow' suggests that the challenge must involve effort be it physical, mental, or both which is why many leisure activities, while enjoyable up to a point, are not very conducive to promoting flow as they are not challenging e.g., watching TV. While the third quote from Csikszentmihalyi perhaps relates most closely to my original assertion that 'your available skills are stretched just enough to provide a challenge'.

When I teach people about flow[33] and how to increase the likelihood of experiencing it, I often recommend that they should try something new, perhaps a different sport, so that they are challenged. But I believe that this is more successful if there is some *transferability* of skills from one sport to another, or from one domain to the other. The reason for this, as already touched upon, is because those who have a higher level of skill are more likely to find flow. My current goal is to challenge myself by learning 'stand up paddle boarding' and I would expect that my high level of alpine skiing skills, in terms of balance, should have good transferability.

Task difficulty and environment

In the sporting arena the environment where the activity takes place has a massive influence on the amount of challenge provided. Extreme sports provide some of the clearest examples of this because of the danger afforded by the environment and the consequences of making mistakes! Sports like wingsuit flying, base jumping, highlining (very high slacklining), free solo climbing, freestyle skiing and snowboarding (half pipe, big air and slopestyle) spring to mind as they often take place in the big mountain environment. But while these are clearly dangerous sports this does not mean that those who

---

[33] The author offers a range of flow workshops including a Flow Coaching qualification. More information can be found on https://www.paralleldreams.co.uk/flow

partake are reckless. On the contrary they are usually highly skilled and incredibly safety consciousness. Nevertheless, there is no doubt that these kinds of sports provide a high level of challenge and are very conducive to flow experiences. Cedric Dumont[34] from Belgium is a wingsuit flyer and Red Bull athlete and a high-performance psychologist. He is a great example of someone who takes 'calculated' risks and regularly experiences flow.

But for mere mortals like myself and those involved in coaching sports it is the clever use of learning zones (as presented in chapter 2) that provides the tool for ensuring that the learner is challenged appropriately (the right amount and at the right time) and therefore more likely to enter a flow state rather than become bored or scared. To recap briefly, the concept of 'learning zones' allows for the task difficulty, skill level, mental strength, emotions, physical effort and the environmental conditions to all be considered and managed so that the learner is put in the appropriate 'zone' be it preparation, comfort, stretch or flow. And while flow is a desirable state to achieve, as part of the learning process, it is neither appropriate nor possible to always be in flow. All of the learning zones are useful, but flow is the one that is hardest to predict or guarantee hence the need for suitably balancing the level of challenge with the level of skill.

---

[34] Cedric Dumont's TEDx Talk "From Fear to Flow" shows how careful professional extreme athletes are:
https://youtu.be/wADq0pb7Nvs

Interaction of the foundations

It would be a misunderstanding to conclude from the descriptions thus far of the three flow foundations that they are completely separate as they clearly impact and interact with each other as can be seen from Figure 9. The model, which I devised while writing this book, featured in one of my blog posts at the time (Tate, 2020a).

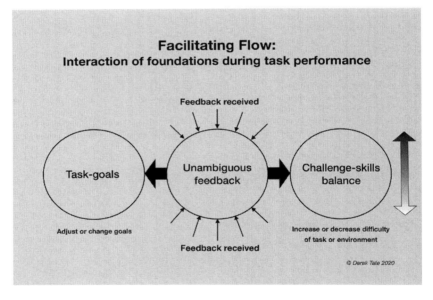

Figure 9.

Unambiguous feedback is central to setting the stage for flow. Because feedback is being received moment-to-moment, in real time, the performer has the opportunity to adjust or change the task goals and/or increase or decrease the difficulty of the task or environment thus adjusting the challenge-skills balance. For example, in skiing the task might be to ski short turns in a specific corridor width, with the goals being to maintain a constant rate of descent and symmetry between left and right turns. Should the environment prove too difficult, because the slope angle is too steep, then the environment could be changed by skiing on a less steep slope thereby reducing the level of challenge. Should the blending of the steering skills prove too difficult then the goal could be adjusted by skiing a slightly wider corridor, which in turn would make the execution of the skills easier. These are just a couple of examples of how immediate feedback can be acted upon to manipulate the other variables in terms of the challenge-skills balance and the task goals. The model presented in Figure 9 can of course be applied to other sports or other domains. So, how would it work for you in your chosen activity?

In conclusion to this chapter, finding flow may well be an elusive experience for some and trying to make flow happen may be akin to the futile pursuit of happiness by focusing on happiness itself. But if you ensure that the three foundations, described in this chapter, are all present then there is a much greater chance that you will experience flow. And as a coach/teacher if you give credence to these foundations, and make them an integral part of your strategy, when working with your learners/performers, then you can create a setting whereby flow can happen. And when it does happen you will experience some or all of the characteristics discussed in the next chapter.

Highlining in Saint Gervais les Bains

CHAPTER 9

Experience the characteristics

Questions to ponder:

⇒ Do you feel in control of what you are doing?
⇒ Do you worry about what others think?
⇒ Do you lose track of time?

The characteristics of flow are the actual mental experiences of the person engaged in the activity. It is important to clarify, at the outset, that not everyone will experience ALL of the characteristics during flow, but these characteristics are what people themselves have consistently reported and they have been very well documented over the years. People who are lucky enough to experience all of the characteristics could be described as having deep flow experiences, which could also be described as an intensely pleasurable altered state of consciousness.

One of the slightly confusing aspects of flow is the inconsistency around the language used to describe both its foundations and characteristics. This became very evident to me during my research and writing of my dissertation. In an attempt to bring some clarity to this I compiled a table (see Table 1) of the different terms used for each of the nine dimensions taken from

Csikszentmihalyi's most well-known books which I believe is helpful in clarifying the scope of the terms denoted in Figure 8 (from the previous chapter) and used as headings throughout these chapters on flow.

Table 1
Flow Dimensions Language Variation Across Texts

Figure 8	Flow in Sports (Jackson & Csikszentmihalyi, 1999)	Flow (Csikszentmihalyi, 1990)	Creativity (Csikszentmihalyi, 1997)	Evolving Self (Csikszentmihalyi, 1993)	Finding Flow (Csikszentmihalyi, 1997)	Running Flow (Csikszentmihalyi, Latter, & Duranso, 2017)	Good business (Csikszentmihalyi, 2004)
Clear goals	Clear goals	Goal-directed	Clear goals every step of the way	Clear goals	Clear set of goals	Clear goals	Goals are clear
Challenge skills balance	Challenge-skills balance	Skills adequate to cope with challenges at hand	Balance between challenges and skills	Personal skills well suited to given challenges	Skills fully involved in overcoming challenge	Challenge-skills balance	Balance between opportunity and capacity
Unambiguous feedback	Unambiguous feedback	Clear clues as to how one is performing	Immediate feedback to one's actions	Immediate feedback	Feedback relevant and immediate	Unambiguous feedback	Feedback is immediate
Focused attention (effortless)	Concentration on the task at hand	Concentration on the task at hand	Distractions are excluded from consciousness	Concentration on the task at hand	Attention becomes ordered and fully invested	Focused attention	Concentration deepens
Action-awareness merging	Action-awareness merging	Merging of action and awareness	Action and awareness are merged	Action and awareness merge	Deep involvement	Merging of action and awareness	The present is what matters
Sense of control	Sense of control	Paradox of control	No worry of failure	Sense of potential control	Happy, strong and satisfied	Sense of control	Control is no problem
Loss of self-consciousness	Loss of self-consciousness	Self-consciousness disappears	Self-consciousness disappears	Loss of self-consciousness	Self-consciousness disappears	Loss of self-consciousness	Loss of ego
Transformation of time	Transformation of time	Time becomes distorted	Sense of time becomes distorted	Altered sense of time	Sense of time is distorted	Distortion of time	Sense of time is altered
Autotelic experience	Autotelic experience	Willing to do it for its own sake	Activity becomes autotelic	Experience becomes autotelic	Worth doing for its own sake	Intrinsic motivation	Intrinsically rewarding

For references to the seven books listed in Table 1 please see the chapter references at the end of this book.

Unpacking the characteristics
What follows is an unpacking of what each of the characteristics means, some examples of how these characteristics relate to different activities, including some personal experiences, as well as highlighting some of the 'flow inhibitors' that might occur and consequently prevent you from being able to get into a flow state.

C1: Focused attention
Attention, focused attention both effortful and effortless has been covered, in great detail, in chapter 3 and as I concluded it is a skill that can be improved through practice particularly with the likes of mindfulness strategies. It is also an area that I will revisit in the next chapter as I reveal what my research uncovered about the transition from effortful to effortless attention.

From the perspective of entering a flow state and experiencing complete concentration on the task at hand it is necessary to be able to block out all distractions that may otherwise use valuable attentional resources.

In today's modern world there are plenty of distractions or rather plenty of things vying for your attention; social media, instant messaging, email and even old-fashioned phone calls! The problem is that some of these 'distractions' become very well-formed habits and things that can be perceived as enjoyable. I am as guilty of this as many other people are. I often find myself wanting to check Facebook, Instagram etc. and can waste quite a bit of time just scrolling the news feed. So, it is important that you develop 'habits' that will encourage better concentration on the task at hand. As I am writing this section, I have put my mobile phone on silent, closed down my web browser and closed Outlook. This certainly increases the likelihood of me getting absorbed in the task at hand and improves my productivity. Irrespective of whether I find flow at least I will feel better about how I have used my time.

But distractions don't just relate to modern technology, they also relate to the demands of modern life and trying to juggle work, family, social activities, leisure, sport etc. It is hardly surprising then that it can be difficult to stay focused in one area when thoughts of other things keep creeping in, and your attention is drawn to all the things that you have on your to do list. The current pandemic has illustrated this more than ever with so many people now working from home. Of course, this has many advantages not least less time wasted travelling to and from work, but the downside is that being at home means there are potentially many distractions from children, pets, your partner etc. and a general lack of structure/control (not to mention space) that can lead to being tempted, or even obliged, to focus your attention elsewhere. It is little wonder then that mindfulness and meditation have become so popular as a way of helping people remain present moment focused. However, this is also the beauty of sport and physical activity and particularly practicing in beautiful outdoor environments. When people come to places like the alps it is much easier to become immersed in both the activity and the environment and to forget (at least for a while) all those other distracting thoughts.

C2: Action-awareness merging

Back in the 1990's I used to deliver a lot of Alpine Ski Leader courses for Snowsport Scotland[35] and one of the slides I used for my off-snow presentations simply said that "thoughts govern action" and I have always loved the simplicity of this. But one of the defining characteristics of flow state is the idea that when action and awareness *merge* there is no separation between thoughts and action and that this gives way to a feeling of oneness. Furthermore, when performing more complex activities there is a sense of ease and effortlessness.

So, in relation to movement and sports, there would appear to be a correlation here between being in the 'performance' stage of skill acquisition (see the DMSA chapter 2) and being able to get to a stage where it is possible to feel a sense of ease and effortlessness. Flow experiences are filled with apparent 'contradictions' and in this case the suggestion is that when you are in flow, and action and awareness merge, that you are not expending a great deal of effort? Yet sometimes best performances come from intense physical and mental effort. Probably a more accurate way of thinking about it would be that you are expending the 'right amount' of effort in order to execute the skill as efficiently as possible. In the late 1980s when skiing became my all-consuming passion, I would watch Ski Sunday[36] on BBC2 (we did not have the luxury of Eurosport in those days) and I remember watching the great Swiss Slalom

---

[35] Snowsport Scotland is the National Governing Body (NGB) for snow sports in Scotland and run a range of coach, leader and instructor qualifications. https://snowsportscotland.org
[36] Ski Sunday is a BBC Sports programme featuring winter sports which originally aired back in 1978 (source Wikipedia).

and Giant Slalom specialist Verni Schneider[37]. My abiding memory is how when she skied her fastest runs, she would look very effortless as if she was not trying so hard. Her smoothness and apparent lack of effort were in fact illustrating efficiency and oneness with the mountain and the snow. This, for me, epitomises the idea of action and awareness merging and is why the term flow is so apt for optimal experience because in sport high-level expert performers exhibit flowing movements that are a pleasure to watch.

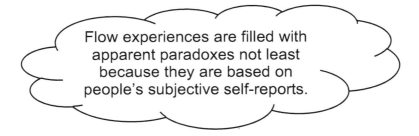

Flow experiences are filled with apparent paradoxes not least because they are based on people's subjective self-reports.

C3: Sense of control

Having a sense of control during task performance comes from trust in your ability (your available skills) and the confidence that when the going gets tough you will have the requisite resources to deal with the situation.

Being in such total control can almost seem contradictory to the freedom that is often talked about when being in flow. I watched a video from the Wimbledon

---

[37] Verni Schneider (Switzerland) is fourth on the all-time female list of World Cup ski racers after Lindsay Vonn (USA), Mikaela Shiffrin (USA) and Annemarie Moser-Proll (Austria).

Championship's Facebook page recently titled "The Trilogy | Becker v Edberg" and one of the comments Boris Becker made when talking about his great tennis rivalry with Stefan Edberg and the difference between winning and losing was that "it was just being free in that moment on the court". So, paradoxically it is that sense of control that allows you to be free!

But what exactly is it that you can control? If you are engaged in an outdoor sport for example you cannot control the weather. The wind might be blowing hard during your round of golf. The visibility might be poor for your slalom ski race. The roads may be wet while cycling. The temperature may be really high, with the sun beating down on you, during a tennis match. And if you are competing against others you cannot control your competitors etc. But what you can control is your own thoughts and actions, and confidence and trust come from practice; purposeful practice that has involved sessions in all kinds of weather conditions and against many different competitors. I remember while working as a trainer/examiner for the British Association of Snowsport Instructors having a student say to me (during an exam), "this is the first time I have skied bumps (moguls) all season". Given that this was late April (and the season starts in December), and that skiing and performing well in bumps was one of the key strands of the exam this did not suggest that the student had taken on the concept that prior planning and preparation prevent [?] poor performance (I left out one of the 'p' words but many of you will know it)! This was clearly a classic example of not practicing with purpose and in itself an inhibitor to potential flow experiences.

C4: Loss of self-consciousness

This is a fantastic benefit of being in flow but conversely being self-conscious is one of the biggest inhibitors to being able to experience flow!

Loss of self-consciousness happens when you are completely immersed in the activity/task at hand. When this occurs, you are not worried about what others may be thinking about your performance.

But it is all to do with the situation and how comfortable you are with the environment in which the activity is taking place and how confident you are about performing the task.

Let me give you a couple of examples from my own experiences, both as a performer and as a ski teacher. The first example relates to public speaking and the lecture I presented at the World Interski Congress in Pamporovo, Bulgaria in March 2019. This was Ireland's lecture and off-snow contribution to this world event. The room was filled to capacity with approximately 90 delegates from all over the world in attendance. Building up to the presentation I was understandably nervous as I seldom speak to such large groups and it was very easy to focus on who my audience were, their depth of knowledge and high standing within the industry. But I was confident and passionate about my subject and I had prepared thoroughly. I knew I had done everything that I could, so my mind was at ease. It was undoubtedly a challenge, but one which I was ready to accept and one which I perceived that I had the skills to cope with. Once I got underway the presentation went very smoothly and I would say that I experienced flow during the talk. I definitely lost my self-consciousness and afterwards I was buzzing with excitement as I had enjoyed the experience so much. Of course, it also helped that other people were very supportive both before and after the presentation and I am very thankful for that.

As a ski instructor, and an examiner of ski instructors, I am very familiar with other people being self-conscious, having a negative perception of their performance and consequently struggling to perform at their best. A classic example of this is when the video camera comes out to capture their performance for subsequent analysis. Immediately many people tend to worry about giving a good enough performance. About getting it right and not making mistakes! About looking good (especially if others, e.g., peers, are going to see the video playback as often happens in ski instructor training sessions). Yet, ironically, the very point of using video is to provide an additional source of feedback to help the learner to see both strengths and weaknesses in their performance. But the mind tends to be drawn to the negative possibilities hence the learner will often tense up and ski less fluidly than they might normally. One solution to this problem is to use the camera regularly enough so that it is not a big thing when performance is recorded. Like everything if you practice frequently enough then it becomes second nature. So, as indicated earlier, you need to become 'comfortable' with the environment and in this instance that includes the video camera. That then frees you up to direct your focus elsewhere be it the equipment (EFA1 - external focus of attention 1), or the terrain in front of you (EFA2 - external focus of attention 2).

C5: Transformation of time

Have you ever been so engrossed in something that the time seemed to pass by incredibly quickly? Maybe it was a project at work, writing an article, running in the outdoors, building a website or solving a difficult maths problem?

Conversely, have you ever been performing a task or well-practiced complex routine and felt like time slowed down? Maybe it was skiing down a wide-open slope with fresh untouched powder, climbing a difficult route, or performing a complex dance routine?

People who experience flow often report time being altered in the two ways I have just described depending on the type of activity they are engaged in. While it might seem paradoxical that time speeding up or slowing down can both happen during flow the common elements are being present moment focused and engrossed in the activity.

Time can also, however, be something that people become obsessed with in a more negative way. Classically at work where an activity is not so enjoyable you may keep checking the clock and counting down the minutes until you are finished for the day with thoughts constantly directed towards what you want to do when you get home. Yet, sometimes it is necessary to keep a check on the time; the ski instructor delivering several lessons in a day will need to be very aware of the time to make sure that the lesson finishes 'on time' and back at the designated meeting point. This in itself requires a great deal of skill and judgement to manage the guest's ability with distance to be covered and ski lifts to be taken.

That is why I personally love full day lessons where there is no time pressure (or very little) making it much easier for my learners to experience flow while engaged in the activity of skiing and for me to experience flow while teaching. So, becoming obsessed with time either through boredom or because it is a requirement of the activity itself can be a real inhibitor to being able to experience flow.

As a slight divergence, or perhaps an addendum, to the experience of time transformation, the Learn, Enjoy, Flow and Grow process is one in which time itself is constantly transformed in a positive way (hence the reason for the 'clock' on the front cover). The LEFG process is both cyclical (clockwise and anti-clockwise) and episodic as each part of your life unfolds, and within that process you have the opportunity to frequently find flow and experience time both slowing down and passing by quickly. Full engagement will allow you to be present more often, to have periods of being mindful and periods of flow with the transformation of time being an indicator of the depth of those flow experiences and the enjoyment that follows.

C6: Autotelic experience

An autotelic experience is one where the motivation is *intrinsic* and where the activity is done for its own sake and the sheer enjoyment that is derived thereof. In other words, when you enjoy something you want to do it more. And because being in flow is both enjoyable during and especially post activity seeking flow can become very addictive. Interestingly, Csikszentmihalyi (1997b) suggests that during a flow experience there is not really the mental space to acknowledge enjoyment and that the real enjoyment, or pleasure, comes after completing the task because, "then we are flooded with gratitude for the excellence of the experience" (p. 32). And the driving force behind these positive emotions comes from the brain producing a chemical mix of neurotransmitters that makes you happy; namely dopamine, oxytocin, serotonin and endorphins. And it is this that can lead to addiction (keeping in mind that addiction can be positive or negative and that obsessive passion is not the desired outcome). Exercise is widely recognised as one of the best ways of producing the 'happy' chemicals therefore combining sport and physical exercise with flow experiences would seem to be a great way to feel good and increase intrinsic motivation.

So, it would seem fairly obvious then, that one of the biggest inhibitors of flow would be a lack of intrinsic motivation or rather where the task is being done for more extrinsic rewards or even worse in order to please others. Parents wanting their children to participate in a particular sport because they themselves enjoy it can sometimes lead to a lack of intrinsic motivation in the child (I'm thinking here of young children being 'put' in ski school rather than them wanting to go)! Equally having to continue in the family business, or keep the family business going, can create a situation where there is little interest and a complete lack of motivation (my wife being a great example of this when she felt trapped in the family sports shop). Now don't get me wrong as I am not suggesting that everyone should always do work that they really enjoy – this is not always possible as sometimes work is a means to an end whereby it funds your leisure time so that you can pursue hobbies and sports that really interest you bringing more meaning to your life. That been said, from my own experience, if you are lucky enough to be able to combine the two and find work that is truly meaningful and enjoyable, and that you would do even if you were not paid for it, then even better.

Flow inhibitors – a recap

The present chapter and the previous have highlighted a number of flow inhibitors and I thought it would be useful to collate and summarise these here at this point. Understanding what can inhibit flow is almost as important as understanding what can facilitate it. Here is a flow inhibitor recap;

1. Over reliance on extrinsic feedback from a coach/teacher etc.
2. Too great a challenge for your available skills resulting in fear and anxiety.
3. Too little challenge resulting in boredom.
4. Distractions from your environment that use up valuable attentional resources.
5. Lack of trust in your ability (available skills) often due to a lack of sufficient practice and preparation.
6. Lack of confidence about performing in certain environments.
7. Being worried about what others may be thinking about your performance.
8. Being obsessed with time and continually checking your watch or the clock.
9. A lack of intrinsic motivation and hence interest in the task.

158   EXPERIENCE THE CHARACTERISTICS

Overcoming the inhibitors of flow means that you need to have the foundations in place, but, crucially, it also requires you to be able to narrow your attentional focus and fully concentration on the task at hand. That is where the link between flow and mindfulness becomes vital so that your attentional energy can contribute to finding flow.

> Understanding what can inhibit flow is almost as important as understanding what can facilitate it.

The destination combined with the activity can transform time.

CHAPTER 10

Flowing with mindfulness[38]

Questions to ponder:

⇒ How do flow and mindfulness work together? Isn't there a contradiction?
⇒ Are there just three foundations of flow?
⇒ Is flow state just an individual experience or can a whole team experience flow?

In the preceding two chapters I have covered, in some detail, both the foundations of flow and the characteristics of flow experiences as subjectively self-reported. Earlier in this book I looked at the importance of mindfulness as part of the 'learning process' and also as a way of remaining in the present with attention deliberately focused on certain stimuli. There is clearly some links between mindfulness and flow but there are also some differences and the two *states* can appear to conflict with each other. So, I will begin this chapter by discussing both synergies and the apparent contradictions.

---

[38] The title for this chapter was inspired by Susan Jackson who first used the title in chapter 9 of the book 'Mindfulness in Positive Psychology' (2016) edited by Itai Ivtzan and Tim Lomas and is used with her permission.

Synergy and contradictions

Purposeful present-moment awareness is a common aspect of both flow and mindfulness and vital for being able to fully focus attention to the task at hand. It is suggested that this key aspect of experiencing flow can be developed through mindfulness practice (Cathcart, McGregor, & Groundwater, 2014; Jackson, 2016b).

While Susan Jackson acknowledges Kennon Sheldon and colleague's (2015) view that the two mind states contradict each other, as flow is all about losing self-awareness through task absorption while mindfulness requires maintaining it, she suggests that they are closely related. Furthermore, she proposes that experiencing flow could be seen as "mindfulness in action" (Jackson, 2016b, p. 152) because there is some similarity between the mental states of both when fully engaged in a task. The suggestion is that mindfulness training, due to its non-judgmental present moment awareness, offers one possible route to facilitating flow (Jackson, 2016b, 2016a).

Therefore, from the points already made it would seem that flow involves effortless attention and the loss of self-consciousness while mindfulness requires self-regulation and maintaining self-awareness. It is also clear, however, that the argument put forward by Kennon Sheldon et al. is based on the idea that both states are difficult to experience at the same time. But this does not negate the possibility that practicing one state, e.g., mindfulness, could better enable the other, e.g., flow or, indeed, that experiencing more flow could lead to greater mindfulness.

Del's[39] research question

Based on everything that I had read about flow, mindfulness and their relationship with sport the burning question that I wanted to try and answer was, "can developing the skill of focused attention for alpine ski instructors while ascending (using ski-lifts), by teaching mindfulness strategies, foster more flow experiences while descending the slopes e.g., performing? And, I guess, by extension could developing the skill of focused attention through mindfulness practices encourage more flow experiences across sport and in life in general?

The study

Project aim: The aim of my study was to find a way, using mindfulness, to develop the focused attention skills of a group of alpine ski instructors during both training sessions and performances in high-pressure environments.

The rationale behind the study was that if you can create more flow experiences for ski instructors, who are training for and taking their exams[40], then there is the potential to increase their overall enjoyment of not only their journey through the certification process, but of their overall participation in the sport and their general well-being.

---

[39] Early on during my time as a trainer/examiner for the British Association of Snowsport Instructors I was nicknamed 'Del' by my great and sadly late friend and fellow trainer Ali Rainback.
[40] Exams refers to snow sports instructor certification pathways offered by national associations such as the Irish Association of Snowsports Instructors. More info on www.iasisnowsports.ie

This could then have a knock-on effect whereby they pass this on to their guests; the general skiing public.

Over my years of being involved in snow sports I have witnessed that ski-lift riding time has the potential to be either a positive or negative experience and that some instructors are much better than others at making it a productive and helpful use of time both for themselves and the guests that they teach. So, the longer-term goal, of my project, was (and is) to enhance the training of ski and snowboard instructors so that they gain the maximum benefit from the time they spend using the ski-lifts and ultimately have more positive experiences as they progress in their ski teaching careers.

The training programme or intervention that I used was introduced back in chapter 3 and I went into some detail about the design and purpose of the Mindfulness Based Skiing Specific Intervention (MBSSI) so please go back to the section 'Training the skill of focused attention' to refresh your memory on this.

The participants for my study were the 10 'alpine skiing' members of the Irish Interski Demonstration Ski Team who were engaged in their build up to the World Interski Congress in Pamporovo, Bulgaria in March 2019. The aforementioned training programme was delivered between November 2018 and March 2019 concluding at the team's final training camp just prior to the event itself which ran from the 16th to the 23rd of March. I chose this group because they were all very high-level *individual* performers who were relatively new to *team* synchronised skiing[41] and because the event itself would involve performing on the world stage in front of many people in what was a high-pressure environment. This was ideal for replicating the kind of pressure that is associated with the ski instructor exam environment. But it also created a beautiful situation where expert level skiers could learn (relatively quickly) the intricacies of team synchronised skiing meaning there would be both a high level of challenge combined with a high level of skill (flow foundation number three).

The design of the research project was in two parts or what in more academic terminology is called mixed methods. The first part (quantitative) was the geeky bit involving questionnaires before and after the training programme to assess the effects on participants flow experiences and in particular their focused attention skills.

The second part was more subjective (qualitative) involving one to one interviews (termed semi-structured) with five of the team members. This provided really rich material about the individuals experiences of the training period as well as the event itself and brought about really interesting findings over and above the effect of the mindfulness training on their ability to experience flow whilst performing.

---

[41] Team synchronised skiing refers to teams of skiers who perform complex routines at national and international events.
https://youtu.be/U1dBNFzN5Z8

The results (part one): So, what were the results and what are their implications for the future of both flow and mindfulness?

Although the sample size (number of participants) was admittedly small (10) the results from the first part of the study were very exciting. Having measured 'overall flow' and the characteristic of 'focused attention' before and after the training period there was a statistically significant increase in the scores of both (see Tate, 2019d for the detailed results). These results supported the original hypothesis that the MBSSI had the potential to help increase overall flow over time, through mindfulness strategies, while riding the ski lifts, and that such training has the possibility of fostering more flow experiences while descending the slopes (i.e., skiing), by developing the skill of focused attention.

As with any scientific study caution should always be exercised. After all, the participants' overriding goal was to improve their performance at synchronised skiing in preparation for the Interski Congress and, while all of the participants were expert skiers, they were not very experienced in the aforementioned discipline of team synchronised performance. It has already been noted that flow (optimal experience) is related to peak performance; hence increasing the participants' propensity to experience flow (through the MBSSI training) may have been a contributing factor in improving their performance. However, the reverse is also a possibility; that improving their performance through tactical and technical coaching and purposeful practice (Ericsson & Pool, 2016) as a team that they were more likely to experience flow, because the foundations to flow (as discussed in chapter 8) were all present when performing. And this may have had more influence than the MBSSI. Without a control condition, it is difficult to say, with any certainty, whether the increase in flow was definitely a result of the mindfulness training programme or some of these other potential factors of the situation. Nonetheless, the results were indeed very encouraging and provided a great foundation from which to look at some of the participants subjective views coming from the interviews.

The results (part two): Six main themes were derived from the five semi-structured interviews that I conducted as follows;

- T1: Focus – maintaining it and losing it
- T2: Usefulness and benefits of the mindfulness training (MBSSI)
- T3: Mindful awareness throughout the journey
- T4: Team bonding
- T5: Emotions – positive and negative
- T6: Feedback and criticism

A summary of these themes follows, but more detailed information is available in my full dissertation[42]. As you will see the results of part two were positive in terms of the participants' perception of improving their focused attention skills, but what transpired was a host of additional and unexpected benefits from their participation in the mindfulness training programme (MBSSI). I have included some quotes from comments that the participants made but for the purposes of

---

[42] Anyone wishing to read the full dissertation should contact me via the Parallel Dreams Coaching Academy website:
www.paralleldreams.co.uk

anonymity they are not attributed to any individual team member.

Theme 1: Focus – maintaining and losing it

Developing the skill of focused attention was obviously a key aim of my study and the interviews explored the participants' level of focus while performing. The kind of words that emerged in relation to focus included: focused attention, engagement, present moment attention, soft vigilance, attention becoming ordered and beam of energy. Interestingly, many of the participants found it easier to focus when they were actually performing at the event itself as opposed to the training camps, as highlighted by one participant:

> "I think that during the training camps it was harder to be focused because I think the whole group had less focus whereas when we were actually there last week it was much easier to be focused because it was there and then, and we had a deadline, we had to do it".

Mental state: This was another aspect of 'focus' that my participants talked about and included the use of, and descriptions about, phrases such as being zoned in/out, dialled in, in sync, on auto pilot, arousal levels, being in a bubble, and experiencing deep involvement. The 'zone' is often referred to as being a very special place that athletes strive to find (Mumford, 2016) and has clear parallels with flow characteristics such as action and awareness merging, sense of control and focused attention. What was evident from the interviews is that some of the participants did find that 'special place' while performing at the event itself. For example, one participant said, "100% focused actually, felt very much like skiing in a bubble down the hill, like I was in my own tunnel vision". While another was so fully immersed in the performances that it was difficult to remember any of the performances on the demonstration slope:

> "I couldn't recollect the run, well, any run on that piste [demo hill Pamporovo] and to an extent it was a blank".

Pre-performance routine: Another aspect of focus that came to the fore related to how the participants used the mindfulness training activities as part of their pre-performance routine. When asked the question about their ability to keep their attention focused during performance the responses often related to those moments just before the performance itself and it was during those moments that quite a bit of effort was required in order to focus their attention:

> "The one thing I do remember is being stood at the top and really my head was going and it must, it was really spinning quite a lot for about 10 seconds and it must have taken a lot of effort to calm that to completely focus that in on the run".

But it was clear that this pre-performance was essential in setting up the performances that followed:

> "I think one complements the other, the pre performance complements the actual performance itself, I think without one you don't have the other".

Conversely during performance one participant said:

> "It's odd because I want to say zero because there was no concentration needed and that sounds odd, but the routine was so dialled in it became really natural, so I wasn't focusing on every turn, or it was as though there wasn't a lot of focus or concentration at that point, it was just going through the motions that you'd already drilled in".

Theme 2: Usefulness and benefits of the mindfulness training (MBSSI)

Participants were asked a number of questions about their experiences using the MBSSI activities as well as whether they felt the training programme had in any way influenced their ability to focus their attention when performing. Through answering these questions, it became evident what 'value' they placed on the programme. It is hardly surprising that the participants' views about individual activities varied, as did their perception as to their usefulness in different contexts. For example, one participant did not find the gratitude ride (the fifth meditative activity) particularly useful during the training camps but found it to be especially beneficial away from the slopes when dealing with some personal life issues. Two of the participants really liked the gratitude ride in the snow sports environment with one commenting:

> "The gratitude ride is quite a nice one because it puts you away from what you're doing at that particular time and puts you in a different place. It's actually quite nice, it can be quite uplifting

when you get off the lift and makes you feel quite good".

Coming back to what was perhaps the key question, as to whether the MBSSI programme had any positive influence on their ability to focus their attention when performing, one participant said that after using the activities:

> "I was a lot calmer you know; I wasn't as excited but calmer for it, not that it wasn't exciting, but I didn't let that excitement get in the way of the performance. I was able to deal with it better".

Another said, "It's turned my normal, the way I would normally get myself going, 180°", referring to how the activities had completely changed their approach to finding that optimal level of arousal and focus for the upcoming performance.

What is clear from the feedback is that the MBSSI activities positively impacted all the participants to a greater or lesser extent, not only with their focused attention skills, but in a variety of ways in either the snow sports environment and/or day-to-day life. This underlines the power of mindfulness training and its many benefits (Baltzell & Summers, 2017).

Open minded: The participant's open-mindedness also had an impact on how beneficial they found the MBSSI activities not least because mindfulness and meditation were 'new' to all the participants that were interviewed. Some embraced the idea fully:

> "I'm very much suck-it-and-see sort of attitude to trying anything that I've not done before".

Those who were more open minded exhibited a desire to learn and to use the opportunity (journey as a team) for self-development. This was beautifully summed up by one participant when referring to the MBSSI communication activities:

> "I think it makes you realise a lot about yourself, so it's a bit of a self-development sort of programme where you highlight your strengths and weaknesses in communication".

Theme 3: Mindful awareness throughout the journey

Awareness is an important aspect of mindfulness and is all about developing greater control over your thought processes which gives you the choice and ability not to react (Ivtzan, 2015). Dan Siegel (2018) talks about mindful awareness as being aware of what is happening without being swept away by thoughts, emotions and judgements. Zig Ziglar (1997) talks about 'reacting' as being negative while 'responding' is positive, and George Mumford (2016) supports this view by saying that when we learn to make choices with a clear and calm mind, we are better able to respond in an appropriate way. The MBSSI programme helped the participants to develop this kind of mindful awareness and gave them the opportunity to 'respond' and make better decisions throughout the journey as they practiced the activities. This participant's quote highlights this point beautifully:

> "I was aware at times where I approached communication in situations in maybe not an ideal way so that kind of led me into different, into the use of the tools slightly differently as well".

Which led to such insights as:

> "...letting go of the fact that what I said was the only way, that my opinion, my thoughts were better than everyone else's".

Association is the key: Mindful awareness also led to more conscious decisions about who to spend time with, particularly when riding the lifts, as prompted by the fifth communication activity 'mindful companions'.

This was evidently one of the most interesting findings from the interviews in so far as how the participants chose to use the activity 'mindful companions'. My thought process behind this activity was that in high-pressure situations such as exams, competitions and events, like the Interski Congress, that participants would choose to spend time with people who helped them to stay positive, thereby potentially avoiding a negative downward spiral. What transpired was somewhat unexpected but showed a great deal of mindful awareness. For example, when one participant was asked the question about consciously choosing your ski-lift companion the answer was:

> "No I actually made a point of, well sorry yes I made a point of trying to go up the lift with different people, but it wasn't to do with the mindfulness stuff, it was more to do with the fact that there was

> a clear A and B team[43] and I wanted to make sure that it wasn't like that so we were all one team if that makes sense?"

Of course, this made perfect sense and it showed a high level of awareness that promoted team bonding and unity (more on this shortly)! It also showed a lack of understanding about what mindfulness is or is not, as this high level of awareness and communion is precisely the aim of mindfulness (Salzberg, 2017). One of the other participants took a similar approach of trying to ride the lift with all of the team members over the course of a day, while two others took the originally expected approach of choosing people that were more positive and uplifting for them. The fifth participant, however, took yet another approach by discovering that the preferred lift companions during training camps were not the same as at the event itself – i.e., during the training camps someone upbeat and jovial was favoured, while at the Interski Congress (where there was greater pressure) the preference was for someone calm and quiet.

Theme 4: Team bonding

Bringing together a group of highly experienced ski instructors, who from their training and experience have developed strong opinions and the ability to work alone and be 'the leader', presented considerable challenge in terms of developing team cohesion and bringing a collection of individuals together as a team in pursuit of a

---

[43] During the training camps the 10-person team skied in two pods of five hence there was a recognition that this could split the unity of the whole team.

common goal (Cox, 1998). One participant echoed this by saying:

> "I'll be honest I found lots of individuals and if we had a, when we had a bad, a poorer performance I found there was, for me, too much chat and too much analysis of what went wrong".

While team bonding was a very evident outcome so too were the challenges that the participants experienced while training and performing together. Developing trust in each other, avoiding conflict, fostering belief in the team, being dependent on others, compromising and finding solutions to overcome problems were all part of the mix of producing a more cohesive team.

For all the participants, performing on the world stage in a synchronised team skiing event was a new experience, and this certainly added to the challenges associated with bringing the team together as illustrated by this quote:

> "I would imagine because it was such a new thing I mean you think you get a group of good skiers together and then all you got to do is ski together that it would be a fairly simple thing but it really wasn't".

Both the communication and meditative activities assisted with this process of bringing the team together even though that was not a specific goal of the MBSSI at the outset. The activities provided a platform or framework so that the participants could use them to overcome some of the challenges and help find solutions:

"...there were certainly moments where [pause] I guess when we had problems or when we were struggling during training that using some of those activities to communicate in a way that I hoped would be well received or wasn't going to create conflict".

Listening mindfully: One of the strongest findings emerging from the interviews was the 'revelation' of really listening to each other, and this carried over to the participants' wider personal and professional lives. It was also a strong factor in helping to build the team. All five of the interviewed participants expressed this sentiment:

"The listening one, I think I've had to work quite hard at".

"Oh, I mean listening was huge to be honest".

"I was listening properly and more mindfully because it's very easy as coaches and instructors to be listening but not actually hearing".

"I actually decided to listen [laughter] a little bit more before I spoke so both wife and three-year-old and yeh it was quite nice actually. I would say it worked out for the better by doing that".

"...towards the end of the camps I was a little bit, I was much more active listening".

Theme 5: Positive and negative emotions

From the interview responses the participants appeared to experience something of an emotional rollercoaster as a result of both the build-up to the Interski Congress and the whole journey that preceded it. The mindfulness training activities helped to bring these emotions to the fore. As mentioned earlier in this book 'emotions' are a big part of positive psychology and have been widely studied with positive emotions initially being seen as most important (e.g., Fredrickson, 2001). Then as the field has developed, the recognition of the value of negative emotions has become equally important (e.g., Kashdan & Biswas-Diener, 2015; Lomas, 2016) and it is without doubt that the participants experienced what could be described as both positive and negative emotions on the road to Pamporovo and that both were a useful part of that journey.

A wide range of emotions were experienced, such as frustration, stress and tedium on the negative end of the spectrum, with calmness, confidence, gratitude, compassion and enjoyment being prevalent on the positive end.

Frustration was more evident on the training camps than the event itself, particularly during group discussions on the mountain, both on the ski-lifts and on the piste[44] as highlighted by one participant:

> "It sounds...but sometimes listening; it was difficult because it was quite long, quite negative in certain

---

[44] Piste, although a French word, is a commonly used term for a marked and patrolled ski run.

> parts of the team and that was quite difficult to listen to".

Stress and pressure were naturally experienced more at the event itself with some of the mindfulness meditative activities being used to help cope with these emotions:

> "Breathing anchor was probably more in terms of when there really was stress and pressure involved like just before some of the runs, especially on the opening ceremony, or the tech demo runs[45], I found the anchor just having something extra to focus on in terms of a part of the body internally, kind of brought me back in from whatever I'd seen outside".

Calmness and serenity were generally seen as very desirable states to experience prior to performance with this tactic being a complete turnaround from one participant's previous approach of getting pumped up:

> "...and actually, this experience has taught me that actually being a bit more calm and serene, and a bit more controlled, was more beneficial for my performance".

Gratitude for the environment was also mentioned:

> "The gratitude ride I really like and just taking in the surroundings, appreciating what's there: quite often don't do that...".

---

[45] 'Tech demo runs' refers to technical demonstrations, which were a requirement of the congress https://youtu.be/IHWCJCuk-W4

All the participants expressed feeling enjoyment, and this is not surprising given that everyone involved on the demonstration team were self-funded and training for and attending the event for themselves (intrinsic motivation). This is beautifully summed up by this quote:

> "The reason I really enjoyed the training and the congress was because it was about me [chuckle] and the focusing on stuff was really refreshing because basically it doesn't happen otherwise".

Theme 6: Feedback and criticism

While the overriding feedback about the mindfulness training programme and its meditative and communication activities was positive there were a number of issues and challenges identified which included questioning their value, resistance to their use, lack of engagement with the programme, lack of time, and not finding some of the activities as useful as others.

Covering the latter first, the mindful observation and mindful hearing meditative activities were the ones that the participants either found most challenging or least useful. One of the main reasons cited for the challenge with the 'observation' was that it was difficult to remain non-judgemental, given that ski instructors are trained to analyse other skiers and snowboarders, which they would invariably see when riding the lift (particularly a surface lift such as a T-bar or drag lift). Prior to implementing the MBSSI training program I tested out the meditative activities on myself and I can concur that the mindful observation was *difficult* for ski instructors as we are programmed to analyse performance. It worked much better when I just looked at a beautiful view in the distance when riding a chairlift or cable car. However, personally I found the mindful hearing to be one of the best activities as I had never realised there were so many sounds to tune into and it was brilliant at keeping me present moment focused.

One of the participants found that the mindful communication activities were not that useful during the training camps but really missed the point that their purpose was to develop the skill of focused attention and useful by-products such as team bonding (as identified earlier in theme 4). Lack of time was also mentioned as a reason for not doing much practice outside of the training camps and while the participants were, indeed, very busy teaching and coaching snow sports this probably had (at least to some extent) more to do with the 'value' or lack thereof that they placed on practicing the activities.

Some participants also found it difficult to concentrate on the mindfulness training activities as well as the technical and tactical training they were doing (there was a lot going on during the training camps). This influenced their lack of engagement with the recorded versions of the meditative activities[46] as they found it awkward to set this up with their phones and headphones before riding the lift. One participant said:

> "I think it was maybe a bit of a tech thing, like it's just less of a faff just to do it as opposed to look

---

[46] The MBSSI guided meditation recordings are available from the Parallel Dreams Coaching Academy's Learning Hub (Documents and Tools): www.paralleldreams.co.uk/learning-hub

through your phone and get it loaded up. I don't know I mean I'm a little bit, sometimes I feel that I'm a little bit old school like I prefer to look at some words written down".

Other factors that may have influenced performance and flow state: There were probably a number of reasons why the team performed as well as it did at the World Interski Congress (based on comments and feedback received from other countries[47]), such as the sheer amount of time they spent training and practicing together and receiving technical and tactical coaching. There is also much to suggest that the mindfulness training programme (MBSSI) assisted with this process, not least because of the framework that the activities provided around which everything else could function. Referring to the MBSSI one participant said:

> "...it wasn't the only thing that helped get us to that stage, but it was, I think it was definitely beneficial to helping us all come together to what we did during our performance day[48]".

Finally, the other factor that needs mentioning that clearly influenced the participants' performance and their ability to zone in and experience flow was 'previous experience'.

---

[47] Some very positive comments were received from leading figures of other participating countries:
www.paralleldreams.co.uk/post/reflections-from-interski-2019-part-1

[48] The 'performance day' referred to was the 20th of March 2019 in Pamporovo when the Irish team were performing technical demonstrations, evening show demonstrations and delivering on-snow workshops and an off-snow lecture.

All of those who were interviewed had some level of experience of performing under pressure in the world of snow sports, e.g., alpine racing, freestyle competitions, ski instructor exams, with some doing this at a very high level. One participant commented, "I had experience of a similar event, so I had that experience with me", while another said, "For the entire thing I was pretty chilled out like I didn't get worked up about anything really", which was a combination of previous experience and that particular individual's personality and high level of confidence.

Mindfulness creates space and choice

Irrespective of using the mindfulness training activities (MBSSI), many of the unexpected benefits were a desirable, even necessary, aim of bringing the team together. One could argue, with some justification, that these outcomes might have been achieved anyway, especially given the prior training and experience of these ski instructors and the skills they had developed, over the years, including communication, leadership and social interaction with guests and colleagues (Carron, Colman, Wheeler, & Stevens, 2002; Turman, 2003). However, what the mindfulness activities achieved was to bring this journey into the realm of consciousness, rather than the automatic, unconscious and reactive world that people often find themselves in.

Mindfulness, by its definition, involves presence, awareness and a non-judgmental approach so that there is space between stimulus and response. The famous quote often attributed to Viktor Frankl (as cited in Baltzell & Summers, 2017, p. 66; Mumford, 2016, p. 76) seems very apt here, "Between stimulus and response there is a space. In that space is our power to choose our response. In our response lies our growth and our freedom". Interestingly, while this quotation indeed beautifully sums up the message Frankl would have conveyed (and basically did convey) before 'mindfulness' was in vogue, it appears that there is no record of him ever saying it, either in his most famous book, *Man's Search for Meaning*, or any of his other writings (e.g., Frankl, 2004, 2012, 2014). But whatever the source, in the context of this discussion it really emphasises that it is this 'space' that allows for choice, i.e., the choice to respond rather than react (as mentioned briefly in Theme 3: Mindful awareness), and that by doing so you promote personal growth.

Amy Baltzell and Joshua Summers (2017) admit that choosing the appropriate response rather than reacting is not always easy, but that it is something that can be learnt through regular mindfulness practice. George Mumford (2016) says that everyone has this calm space inside them, and mindfulness helps find that place. It would appear, from the results of my study, that the regular mindfulness practice that the participants engaged in allowed them to create this 'space', which in turn led to their personal growth, as identified by the participants themselves, e.g., see final quote that concludes this discussion. The range of information that came from those interviewed, and the subsequent six themes that emerged from the data, illustrate the benefits that accompanied this growth. With the primary goal of developing the skill of focused attention achieved, the additional benefits can be summarised as:

- how easily the mindfulness activities could be integrated into a pre-performance routine;
- how the activities could be adapted to other life contexts to impact and benefit day-to-day life;
- the importance of truly listening;
- that association (choosing your companions) is the key both in training situations and in everyday life;
- how the activities positively influenced the whole social dynamic within the team, ultimately creating unity, trust and belief in each other and the team as a whole.

A final quote from the interviews sums up this discussion nicely:

> "I think the only other thing to add is that it's been interesting to see the others change throughout the training, and throughout the week that we had last week [at the Interski Congress]. They've all been on quite a long journey and we have seen, or I have seen, quite a bit of change in the individuals and their personalities as well, which is a positive thing"

Overall learning from my research
Having covered the results of each part of my research what follows is the more major outcomes and how these might contribute to the field of flow research and their implications for you, the reader, if you are seeking more flow in your life.

More flow

The results of the pre-post comparison of questionnaires, combined with feedback from the five interviews (particularly in relation to Theme 1: Focus), suggest that the participants on my study had more flow experiences while performing during their final training camp in Bulgaria and at the Interski Congress itself, when performing on the world stage, than they had experienced before the commencement of the mindfulness training.

However, as suggested at the outset of chapter 9, not everyone will experience **all** of the six characteristics of flow in any given flow episode and the dimensions of transformation of time (ToT) and loss of self-consciousness (LoSC) have tended to be more elusive.

For example, while it would appear that ToT was part of the flow experience for some of my participants the diversity of language and descriptions they used to describe their mental state (see Theme 1) indicates that they may have experienced flow in different ways and with varying degrees of intensity.

Attention can be trained

One of the key findings of the research was that 'attention' can be trained. Of course, you may be thinking that this is not an earth-shattering piece of news, and it has already been alluded to in part one of this book, and specifically in chapter 3 – 'Training the skill of focused attention'. Nevertheless, the results of the quantitative part of the study in relation to the flow characteristic of focused attention combined with feedback from the interviews provide additional support for this opinion. Furthermore, mindfulness when used as a training strategy appears to be an excellent vehicle for achieving this goal.

Unlike other studies that have used mindfulness interventions to foster flow (e.g., Aherne et al., 2011; Kaufman et al., 2009) this study homed in on the specific 'skill' and 'characteristic' of focused attention with the MBSSI's primary goal to use its activities (meditative and communication) as a strategy for developing attentional skills. While additional benefits were derived as well, both for the individuals and the team as a whole, the significant results support the idea that attention can be trained by using mindfulness-based techniques. Dan Siegel (2018) talks about there being three pillars associated with training the mind, the first of which is focused attention (the others being 'open awareness' and 'kind intention'), while Amy Saltzman (2018) offers a host of practical mindfulness-based activities for developing attention skills, and the whole basis of the Mindfulness Meditation Training in Sport programme (MMTS 2.0: Baltzell & Summers, 2017) is about training the mind and improving attention, reinforcing that this type of training is becoming more commonplace in the sporting arena.

Effortful and effortless

What also transpired from my study was that the type of attention experienced by the participants varied and could be described as both effortful and effortless. Christian Swann and colleagues (2017) proposed the existence of an overlapping state of optimal performance in sport, that can be experienced as well as flow, which they have termed the 'clutch' state. It is proposed that this 'clutch' state is more about *making* it happen (e.g., effortful) whereas flow is more to do with *letting* it happen (e.g., effortless). Swan et al. proposed a new and integrated model that combines the dimensions of flow and clutch states with some being common to both – e.g., absorption, altered perceptions and enjoyment – but with some unique to each state – e.g., **flow:** effortless attention, loss of self- consciousness and critical thoughts; **clutch:** deliberate focus with intense effort. They also suggest that the outcome of each state is slightly different with clutch leading to exhaustion, while flow is more energising. Finally, they suggest that an athlete can move from one state to the other during a performance depending on whether their goals are 'open' and more exploratory (hence flow) or more 'fixed' towards a specific outcome e.g., being within sight of winning (hence clutch).

These two states could go some way towards explaining the controversy about whether attention in flow is effortful or effortless; however, the evidence from my study – in terms of the feedback from the participants interviewed – indicated that, in the context of performing team synchronised skiing, the participants moved from more effortful attention (feasibly clutch), in the moments just before starting each run, to more effortless attention once the run was underway (flow). So, perhaps, then, the type of attention applied/experienced evolves through pre-performance to actual performance from more effortful to more effortless? Assuming this to be the case then, and picking up on the relationships between flow and mindfulness from the beginning of this chapter, this could go some way towards understanding the 'contradictions' between the two states (flow and mindfulness) and how practicing effortful attention in mindfulness can lead to, or encourage, effortless attention in flow.

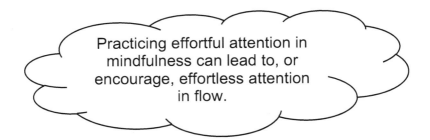

Daniel Kahneman (2012) proposes that there are two systems in the mind with *System 1* being automatic, quick and reactive with little or no effort and no sense of voluntary control, while *System 2* allocates attentional resources to demanding and effortful tasks, while maintaining self-control, in order to avoid distractions and temptation. He says, "as you become skilled in a task, its demand for energy diminishes" (p. 35); however, it requires effort to prepare for a task.

These points certainly tied in with the experiences of the participants in my study, and their feedback in relation to needing more effort in the moments just prior to the performance. But it still begs the question, which system is being engaged when in flow? The suggested answer to this is that there are two kinds of attention: the first being about concentration on the specific task (absorption) and the second being deliberate control of attention (self-control) to override distraction and temptation which exacts a psychological cost (Schmeichel & Baumeister, 2010). So, a person in flow becomes so absorbed in the task at hand that no attention is used up, or needed, for controlling thoughts or avoiding distraction. But this still appears to suggest that there is a conscious element to focusing on the task at hand meaning that it is not entirely System 1 that is engaged when in flow?

Possibly the answer lies in the distinction between external and internal focus of attention. Gabriele Wulf and Rebecca Lewthwaite (2010), whom I introduced back in chapter 3, conducted and reviewed several studies that suggest an external focus of attention requires less mental and physical effort. By focusing on the outcome (movement effect) rather than the input (body movements) greater automaticity is promoted leading to more efficient, effective and economical performances (see also BEE Focused in chapter 3). So, it would seem feasible that both System 1 (automaticity of body movements) and System 2 (conscious focus on movement effect and external cues) are involved when a person is in flow as "control of attention is shared by the two systems" (Kahneman, 2012, p. 22).

Practice, and more specifically deliberate practice (Ericsson & Pool, 2016), leading to expertise, also appears to play an important role in whether the attention required in flow is perceived as effortful or effortless. Fredrik Ullen, Orjan de Manzano and colleagues (2010) propose that the attention – or "high attention" (p. 205) as they describe it – required in flow is different from the type of attention required during mental effort. Because expertise leads to automaticity in the execution of a skill, attentional resources can be shifted away from motor processes to "more qualitative aspects of motor output" (p. 209) such as speed and accuracy of movements. This would seem to add further support to the earlier discussion and the idea that the participants in my study, due to their high level of skill and being well practiced at the synchronised routines, were able to shift their attention to more external cues during performance and away from motor processes involved in executing technique (mental effort) therefore leading to more effortless attention and flow experiences.

A proposed new model of flow

One of the criticisms of the flow construct is the confusion surrounding which dimensions are foundations and which ones are outcomes of the experience e.g., characteristics – a point well made by Rene Weber (2019) during the Flow Symposium that I attended at the Max Planck Institute for Imperial Aesthetics in Frankfurt in June 2019. Given the preceding discussion and the findings from my research study (in particular the subjective experiences of the participants) I sought to question my conceptualisation of the original model of flow (see Figure 8, in chapter 8) and consequently propose a new model of flow with 10 dimensions (see Figure 10):

FLOWING WITH MINDFULNESS

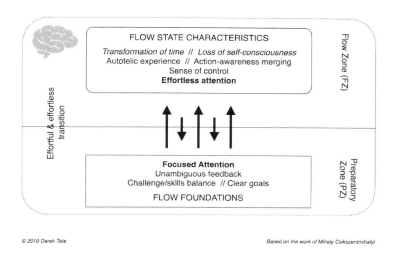

Figure 10.

The basis of this new model, titled "The Fluctuating Attention Model of Flow", is that the 'attention' dimension is split into two separate dimensions with 'focused attention' (effortful) being a foundation of flow (and closely aligned to the attention required in mindfulness), while 'effortless attention' is a characteristic (process outcome). In line with the findings of my study, the attention moves from effortful to effortless (big arrows) as flow state is experienced; however, it is recognised that a person who moves into the flow zone (FZ: across the effortful and effortless transition) can return to the preparatory zone (PZ: little arrows) should attention become more effortful as highlighted earlier in clutch state (Swann et al., 2017), System 2 (Kahneman, 2012), mental effort (Ullen et al., 2010) or where the attentional cues move from external to internal (Wulf & Lewthwaite, 2010).

An example of the proposed new model in action could be seen from one participant's interview feedback where they talked about the effort required in the final moments leading up to the performances at the World Interski Congress (PZ: Focused Attention) and said that during the performance itself they became so fully immersed that they could not remember any of the performances on the demonstration hill at the congress (FZ: Effortless Attention). However, another participant spoke about the difficulty of maintaining focus during the training camps suggesting that their attention fluctuated between the preparatory and flow zones.

Based on this new model the flow foundations from chapter 8 increase from three to four with the fourth being F4: Focused attention. While the characteristics covered in chapter 9 remain the same except that C1 changes from Focused attention to Effortless attention.

Foundations revisited

So, just to recap, as previously emphasised, the three flow foundations need to be in place in order to encourage the likelihood of experiencing flow and they are ALL controllable e.g., as coaches/teachers (and indeed participants) you can set clear goals; you can develop the skills to be able to notice and use feedback in the moment in relation to those goals; and you can adjust the level of challenge so that the available skills are slightly stretched. But, now, this new fluctuating attention model of flow (Figure 10) introduces a fourth foundation of focused (effortful) attention that is also controllable not least because it is trainable through practices like mindfulness. Therefore, it is my assertion that by having **all four** of these foundations in place the chances of experiencing flow will increase further.

> Having ALL FOUR flow foundations in place (rather than three) further increases the chances of experiencing flow.

Figure 11 (which now supersedes Figure 9 from chapter 8) takes this development into account and shows how these four foundations work together *during* the performance of a task.

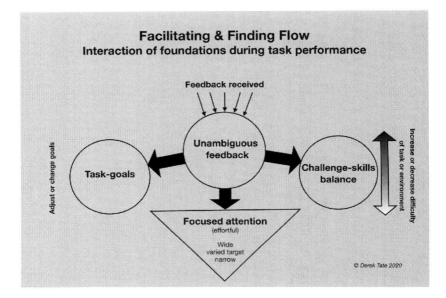

Figure 11.

Building on the earlier foundations model this updated version emphasises how unambiguous feedback also impacts the fourth foundation of focused attention. The performer can use this moment to moment intrinsic feedback to intentionally (with effort) direct their attention to certain stimuli (varied target – mindful learning) and this attentional focus may be wide or narrow depending on the activity and goal.

By using, and acting on, feedback received during task performance to influence the other three foundations, the performer can become fully immersed and engaged in the task at hand thus increasing the chance of attention transitioning from effortful to effortless and moving from the preparatory zone into the flow zone.

Team flow

A more recent development in flow research is team flow. The majority of research, to date, has focused on the individual but the idea of 'teams', be it in business or sport, finding a collective flow state is exciting. In reality, this already happens (but has not been studied to any extent). You just have to look at sports like football (soccer for our USA readers) where the whole team is completely focused on the combined goal and have a breadth of attention and heightened awareness so they know exactly where each other team member is positioned without even having to seemingly look at each other. This kind of attention and awareness was evident with the Irish Interski Team during their performances at the World Interski Congress and with the way that they dialled in their routines. Team flow itself was not measured so I can only hazard a guess that it was happening, but it would be interesting to measure it in the future with synchronised skiing demonstration teams.

Nevertheless, I can reflect on the training and performances of the Irish Interski Team in relation to the work of Jef van den Hout, Orin Davis and Bob Walrave (2016) who suggest that creating team flow works on the same basis as individual flow in that certain foundations need to be in place before the team can experience flow.

These are as follows;

1. Having a collective team goal.
2. Ensuring that individual goals are aligned to the team goal.

3. A high-level of skills amongst the team that are combined while allowing the use of individual strengths (see Linley & Bateman, 2018).
4. Open communication and feedback across the team.
5. A mentally safe place where people can perform without fear of failure. Clearly there are degrees of failure that can be tolerated but effective learning will only take place where mistakes are allowed.
6. A shared commitment to achieving that common goal which requires dedication from all.

These six foundations resonate strongly with how I witnessed the Irish Interski Team working together.

And van den Hout, Davis and Walrave suggest that the characteristics of team flow include;

1. A holistic focus (total concentration on the shared activity).
2. A sense of unity (not feeling self-conscious with each other).
3. Trust in each other (which largely comes from open communication and feedback).
4. A joint sense of progress towards the common goal.
5. Shared intrinsic motivation as a result of shared values.

These characteristics were certainly not present when the Irish Interski Team began their training for the World Interski Congress, but the themes derived from the interviews and some of the team member's quotes suggest that many of these team flow characteristics were indeed developed as the training progressed and during the congress itself in Pamporovo.

Summarising flow

Wow what an incredible ride it has been so far in this book. I appreciate that this section, about flow, has been very detailed and has hopefully given you a good understanding of what flow is and how to encourage it in your own life, and as a coach/teacher how to facilitate it for others. I have looked at the research underpinning flow, including my own, and clarified what are its foundations and what are the characteristics that are experienced. I have also looked at the concept of team flow which builds on individual experiences. There is no doubt in my mind that it is an extremely exciting time right now for flow psychology with many people researching it and even more wanting to experience it.

Flow helps you get more enjoyment from what you do and this in turn increases motivation and interest. Flow helps make learning more robust and can even speed up the process. As I have already mentioned the LEFG method is cyclical in both directions (clockwise and anti-clockwise) and in many ways' 'flow' is the holy grail so to speak. If you can experience it regularly it enhances learning and enjoyment, but it also promotes growth because of the sense of achievement which follows, which then leads to a stronger self-concept and moving beyond the ego and this is what part four of the book is all about. So, read on and find out how you can grow and by doing so bring greater purpose, hope and meaning to your life.

Team synchro skiing

PART FOUR
GROW

"What a man can be, he must be. This need we call self-actualization"

Abraham Maslow

CHAPTER 11

Discover your purpose

> Questions to ponder:
>
> ⇒ What does having a purpose mean?
> ⇒ Do your activities align to your purpose?
> ⇒ Should you feel pressured into discovering purpose?

The final chapters of this book are all about growth – your growth – or self-actualisation as Abraham Maslow talked about.

My own growth has led me to discovering my purpose and just as the achievement of long-term goals are a result of enduring passion (as I discussed in chapter 5) so too can discovering your *purpose* be a result of engaging in that passion.

My purpose has developed over my life to date. All of my interests have woven together to create a bigger purpose. Let me try to explain my thinking;

As I reflect, I can see how my different interests and chapters within my life have fitted together like pieces of a jigsaw puzzle. Now I'm not convinced that the jigsaw will ever be completed, but the picture is starting to reveal itself.

As a child at primary school, football (soccer) was my thing. I played for the school team and the Cub Scouts' team (with the latter being a very successful team, mainly down to a great coach called Tommy Ticher). The team aspect was something I enjoyed, but I loved outdoor exercise and sport in general. When I was 11 years old, karate became my sport and I loved the rigorous practice and discipline that it fostered. But I also liked the spiritual side (although not in a religious sense). Then in secondary school, unlike many pupils, I loved physical education. It was probably the combination of fitness, trying different sports and being outdoors – I even liked cross country running! Secondary school was also a time where through Geography I started to become fascinated with mountains and in particular the alps. I'm not sure, at that stage, that I could see any connection between mountains and my love of sport!

Skiing then entered my life and provided another opportunity for rigorous practice and being outside but this time in the mountains. As time went by the sheer awe of the alps and the spiritual side that this emotion evoked were additional benefits to this new sport. Of course, there was also the thrill of speed and the feeling of freedom that skiing afforded.

Growing up, in school, I was incredibly shy and the thought of standing up and speaking to a group of people filled me with terror. But my love of skiing helped me to overcome that fear as I became a ski instructor and started to share this love with others. Teaching skiing helped me grow by giving me confidence, not only in myself but also because I could help others gain enjoyment from my sport and the environment.

It would be fair to say that initially my real passion was the sport of skiing, both as a participant and as a teacher, but as I said back in chapter 5 I soon realised that my true passion was, in fact, living in the alps and everything that goes with that lifestyle and skiing was just one part of that.

There are clearly lots of little connections between each of my interests which led me on my journey to living in the alps and through engaging in this passion – finding a partner to share this life, running our own ski school, skiing, ski touring, hiking in summer with and without our dogs etc. – I have discovered my purpose and that is to share and promote the health and well-being benefits that come from this kind of lifestyle in the mountains. Our Parallel Dreams Coaching Academy's tagline really does sum up my purpose: "health and well-being through sport and mountain life", with the caveat that this means sharing that with as many people as possible. And delivering a variety of courses, workshops, conferences etc., through the Academy and our ski school help me to enact my purpose.

Therefore, from my own life example, I would say that discovering your purpose takes time. Let your interests shape your purpose. Having long-term goals is important but you should not be completely rigid with these. Things change over time, and new and unexpected interests will develop but they may simply be another piece of the jigsaw. I sometimes think back to my karate days and regret not completing my then goal of black belt (I achieved one below – brown belt), but then I think how much that time prepared me for the future chapters in my life, not least, the discipline of rigorous practice and spirituality. The MAPP course at University helped me to realise how this journey has unfolded and has given me much greater clarity about my purpose. Remember that passion is the emotional fuel that drives you (quite often to what you want) but purpose is much bigger and is more about discovering what you are here to do, and to be, and how you can help others.

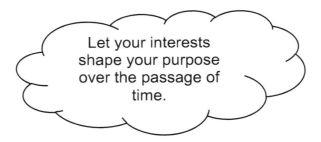

Let your interests shape your purpose over the passage of time.

Unlike some of the previous chapters, in this book, where I have often looked at the research and science and defined important terms before giving some examples of people who illustrate these things, in this chapter I will build on my own example of discovering my purpose by introducing you to Martin Drayton and then seeing how our pathways to *purpose* match up to some of the theory!

Martin lives in Utah in the USA and is a passionate snowboarder. He started snowboarding back in 1985 inspired by the French 'Apocalypse Snow' videos[49]. His solid background in skateboarding helped him to quickly

---

[49] These movies started the snowboarding revolution in Europe: https://youtu.be/rbdUEOyryeg

become proficient (transferable skills). He achieved his first on-snow snowboard instructor qualification with the Austrian Vöss Association[50] in 1987 and then proceeded to write the British Snowboard Association (BSA) teaching manual for snow-based courses. He was then selected to be one of the small group of BSA and BASI[51] teachers to work together to set up the BASI snowboard qualification pathway co-authoring the on-snow manual. He was very much one of the pioneers of the sport in the UK.

He went on to serve as a BASI Snowboard Trainer and Examiner for over 20 years until the transatlantic expenses became too great having moved to the USA in 1999. He has been a trainer in Park City, Utah where he lives year-round for the last 20 years. He currently teaches part time as his full-time job is as a flight attendant.

He has raced slalom, giant slalom and boardercross up to World Cup level and still races as an amateur having won the US National boardercross titles at Masters level. He finished fourth out of a field of 100+ racers in the 2019 World Airline Championships Boardercross at the age of 59! He is particularly proud of the fact that the other finalists were 30 years younger.

With regards to discovering his purpose Martin says, "my purpose, I feel, is two-fold. Firstly, to help advance and

---

[50] Founded in 1987 Vöss – the Association of Austrian Snowsurfers – was later renamed the Austrian Snowboard Association (ASA).
[51] BASI – the British Association of Snowsport Instructors would at that time have used the term 'Ski Instructors' rather than 'Snowsport Instructors'.

promote the sport, as much as possible. Secondly, I am, as an athlete of colour, trying to break the stereotypes that exist in our sport. Winter sports in general are perceived as the domain of wealthy white males, and it need not be. There are athletes of diverse racial and ethnic backgrounds, from various socio-economic backgrounds, that have the ability to compete at the highest levels, given the opportunity and support. Women too, are grossly underrepresented in our sport" (a point echoed by me in one of my blog articles; Tate, 2020e).

In terms of his activities aligning to his purpose he says:

> "I have been a spokesperson for snowboarding since the early days, appearing on several television programs, and working as a presenter, in an effort to educate people on the sport. I have also written many technique and educational articles published in the ski press.
>
> By using my expertise to train future instructors and instilling in them a sense of pride and professionalism in what they do, I am trying to leave a legacy that ensures the continued growth of the sport.
>
> I am currently heavily involved in helping develop Diversity and Inclusion initiatives at both my local resort (the largest in the US), and at the national level with the Vail Corporation. Also, by competing and winning, at both national and international level, I have proven without doubt, that you truly shouldn't judge a book by its cover".

Purpose or calling?

Reflecting on Martin's story, and that of my own, I am struck by the thought of whether the term *purpose* is correct or whether it should be *calling*? Are they the same thing or is trying to differentiate these two terms simply being a little pedantic?

Thomas Moore (2009) says, "a calling is the sense that you are on this earth for a reason, that you have a destiny, no matter how great or small" (p. 17). Now this may all sound rather theatrical, like something from a fantasy world like Lord of the Rings where Frodo Baggins becomes the ring bearer and his *calling* is to destroy the One Ring in the fires of Mount Doom where it was forged and by doing so save the world from the dark Lord Sauron. But what about mere mortals? What about the real world? How many people could actually say that they have a calling? Perhaps not very many, but Moore does say that this calling can be great or small, so it does not have to be something that necessarily saves the world!

But is a calling and a purpose one in the same? Scott Barry Kaufmann in his recent book Transcend (2020) has studied the works of Abraham Maslow (probably in more depth than any living person) and says that, "Maslow often wrote about purpose as akin to having a calling" (p. 156) noting that a calling is often associated with religion even though this does not have to be the case. Kaufmann himself says, "the need for purpose can be defined as the need for an overarching aspiration that energizes one's efforts and provides a central source of meaning and significance in one's life" (p. 154). What I am particularly struck by here is that Kaufmann is suggesting that human beings *need* to have a purpose because that is what gives them energy and provides meaning in their lives (more on this in the final chapter). Furthermore, he says that, "science confirms that seeing one's work as a calling is related to satisfaction in life" (p. 156) and this links back to my earlier point, or rather question, about how many people in the real world could actually say that they have a purpose of a calling? As I said, probably not that many, but what this indicates is that you should because by doing so you can, as a by-product, find much greater happiness and contentment. And this is a much better route to happiness than the futile pursuit of happiness itself.

So, from the discussion so far, a calling could be perceived as being something even bigger than a purpose but there is also much in common between the two terms. Returning to Martin's story and his 'work' in snowboarding it appears that participating, competing, teaching and promoting the sport has been much more than a job or even a career. It does seem to have become an overriding purpose, and even calling, to use the sport, and his position within it as a role model, to develop diversity and inclusion. I don't know for sure but I would guess that the second aspect of his purpose, relating to being an athlete of colour and breaking the existing stereotypes, is a role that he has grown into and has therefore been part of discovering his purpose or even realising the positive influence that he can have.

For me, I would say that my purpose is not something that I had when I was in my 20s doing many winter seasons as a ski instructor. Back then it was a job that I very much enjoyed (not to mention all the partying lifestyle that went with it) but as I grew into the job I began to realise the benefits of the lifestyle, and the environment, and how I was able to share that with others by helping them to become lifelong enthusiasts of the sport. And this simply grew to a bigger sense of purpose as I helped other people forge similar careers in snow sports. And now, today, my calling is to help as many people as possible experience the health and well-being benefits of sport and mountain life whatever their level of participation or involvement.

Could it be that discovering your purpose is a journey and for some that journey may be short, while for others it may be long? It may involve having a 'job' that becomes a 'career' and then becomes a 'calling' (purpose). If you are lucky enough to have a job that interests you, challenges you and that you enjoy and involves flow experiences, then the likelihood of it transforming into something bigger, in terms of purpose, is greatly increased. But everyone's journey will be different, and the important thing is to allow it to unfold, to listen to your inner voice and be flexible in your goals.

Dan McAdams (1993) says that, "human beings are storytellers by nature" (p. 27). The mind creates a narrative for each episode and chapter within the journey of life and if these stories are considered to be 'truth' then they become your personal myth. It is perhaps unsurprising then that your purpose will take time to develop because the passage of time is necessary for creating your own personal myth and for making sense of life. McAdams says that "mature identity requires that we leave a legacy that will, in some sense, survive us" (p. 37). Therefore, with age comes a certain sense of urgency to find your purpose so that you can leave something behind you. Martin spoke about this when he said, "I am trying to leave a legacy that ensures the continued growth of the sport". And my writing of this book (and other works) aligns perfectly with my purpose to share with others health and well-being through sport and mountain life.

Values-based purpose

Assuming that you have discovered your purpose, it is important to consider that this alone by no way ensures personal growth especially if your goals are ethically suspect. History is littered with people who have been very successful at the expense of others, across many domains such as politics, business and sport, therefore your purpose needs to be underpinned by sound morals and values such as honesty, respect, courage, forgiveness, humility, generosity, compassion, fairness, determination etc. Of course, there is much debate about which morals or values are more important and the preceding list is by no means exhaustive. You may also be thinking that morals and values are not necessarily the same thing; morals are more about what society expects of you, while values are your personal beliefs based on those morals. But morals in different societies across the world will vary increasing the need for 'respect' of not just the individual but also of different cultures.

In positive psychology Christopher Peterson and Martin Seligman (2004) were instrumental in classifying strengths of character (which I touched on back in chapter 1) based on moral virtues. They undertook a massive task to establish 'virtues' that were universal (or at least widely recognised) across different cultures, religions and socio-economic backgrounds involving an extensive literature review and thematic analysis of all the data. The six core virtues that were derived were; courage, justice, humanity, temperance, transcendence and wisdom. These then formed the basis of the 24-character strengths of the VIA Institute on Character[52]. It would seem only sensible then that your purpose in life should be grounded in the virtues that underpin strengths of character.

Self-actualisation

So, what does purpose have to do with self-actualisation?

Let me first unpack what is meant by the term. There are many definitions of 'self-actualisation' but it is largely attributed to Abraham Maslow (1943), and his Theory of Human Motivation, being the highest of the human needs and the desire to realise your full potential doing what you are 'here' to do. The Cambridge Dictionary online defines it as "a person's desire to use all their abilities to achieve and be everything that they possibly can". Maslow himself famously said, "what a man can be, he must be" (p. 382). Hence if you cannot fulfil your potential within the areas of your life that you enjoy, and that you are good at (strengths), then it is likely that you will become restless and discontent.

Scott Barry Kaufmann (2018) looked at what it means to be self-actualised in modern times especially given that Maslow's original Theory of Human Motivation was published way back in 1943! He carried out a rigorous

---

[52] The VIA Institute on Character allows you to discover your strengths and provides a free online survey. Go to https://www.viacharacter.org to take the test.

study using a number of well-known measures of personality and well-being to show that Maslow's original 10 characteristics of self-actualising people (Maslow, 1950) do indeed have relevance to life in the 21st century. Of particular interest to this chapter was the characteristic of purpose. It should be stressed that being strong in any *one* of the 10 characteristics does not necessarily indicate a person who has become self-actualised but scoring highly in a number of the characteristics would suggest that this is more likely to be the case. Therefore, a 'values-based purpose' as discussed earlier would mean that a number of the other characteristics are met e.g., acceptance, authenticity, humanitarianism and good moral intuition.

In conclusion to this chapter I would say that discovering your purpose takes time and the need for purpose increases with age as leaving a legacy comes to the fore. But your purpose must be based on good moral values which in turn will lead to exhibiting many of the characteristics of a self-actualised person.

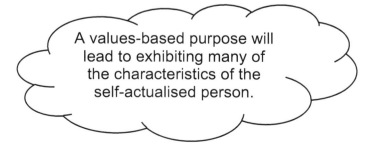

DISCOVER YOUR PURPOSE

Alpine skiing – boot packing

CHAPTER 12

Simply be

> Questions to ponder:
>
> ⇒ Are you a human being?
> ⇒ Does 'being' promote good mental health?
> ⇒ What about your ego?

It's late at night as I ponder what it means to 'simply be'. Through this writing process I have often found that my thoughts keep formulating through the night and sometimes I even need to get up in the early hours and write things down in case I forget them by the morning. The irony here is that my mind is busy when perhaps it should be quiet? I am now an avid meditator and habitually do a short session of meditation before I go to sleep. For me it calms my mind, or at least allows for a 'pause' before it starts working again at processing my thoughts and ideas. So, in terms of my own personal growth, is this the right course of action? I'll come back to this shortly but here are some of my late-night ponderings;

Human being or human doing?

Do you want to be remembered for being or doing? For who you were or what you achieved? Do you want to be remembered for being a good wife/husband, sister/brother, parent, for being kind, compassionate, fun to spend time with, generous, for helping others? Or do you want to be remembered for what you achieved, the books you wrote, the things you changed/influenced, the difference you made, for what you created? Well if I'm honest I would say that it is a mixture of the two. I want to be remembered for being a 'human being' but I also want to be remembered for some of my achievements. For what I did. In short, it would be nice to be remembered rather than simply pale into insignificance. It is, after all, not so much the life you live as the life that's in the years that you live. It is much better to live a full life in whatever time you have rather than just trundle along and get by.

Yes, there is no doubt that we are human beings BUT we are also human doings. The problem is that we get so caught up in 'doing', especially in this modern world full of technology, that we forget to be. We rarely make time to simply be.

However, as with so many things in life it is all about balance and the message of this book has consistently been that each individual's path through the LEFG process will be unique. So, I too must continue to find what works for me, but I have definitely found that making time to stop doing and spend more time being is very beneficial whether that's a short meditation before bed or being more mindful during the day.

Mental health vs. mental illness

Too much 'doing' can certainly lead to stress and if unchecked may develop into rumination, anxiety, burnout etc. Such a downward spiral could then take you into the realm of mental and possibly physical illness.

Mental health is extremely topical these days and quite rightly so, but the context surrounding the language used creates a good deal of confusion and misunderstanding. The term 'mental health' is too often used when referring to poor mental health or mental illness! Simply type the term 'mental health' into Google and most of the results will relate to mental disorders, problems and illness. And even if the definition begins by referring to emotional, psychological and social well-being the information quickly moves onto problems with thinking, mood and behaviour etc., e.g.,
https://www.mentalhealth.gov/basics/what-is-mental-health

Compare this with the term 'physical health' where the majority of the information, from an internet search, is about things that you can do, and focus on, in order to improve your physical health e.g., lifestyle, level of physical activity, fitness programmes, sport, diet, nutrition, and gut health as well as the cessation of bad habits such as smoking and control of too much alcohol consumption.

Society and the media still have a long way to go to get over the stigma associated with 'mental illness' when compared to having a physical illness or disease despite many of the great initiatives being championed by high profile personalities from various walks of life including sport.

And this is why positive psychology has become so important, particularly with the advent of the second wave or PP 2.0, as it is known, which takes a more realistic view by embracing the challenges and difficulties of life while striving for greater well-being (Ivtzan, Lomas, Hefferon, & Worth, 2016). Wouldn't it be nice if when typing in the term 'mental health' you were instead given lots of results pointing to things you can do to improve your mental health such as; positive emotions, mindfulness activities, meditation, yoga, seeking flow etc. (many of which encourage you to be a human being – at least in terms of remaining present moment focused – rather than a human doing). After all mental health may be the absence of mental illness but this in no way guarantees good mental health (Seligman, 2011). What is important to clarify here is that 'mental health' can be discussed in terms of good mental health or poor mental health (Tate, 2020d) and in positive psychology the idea of a mental health continuum ranging from languishing (poor) to flourishing (good) has been widely written about (Keyes, 2002, 2007).

So, I like to think of good mental health being about moving from 'zero to flourishing' and finding time to simply be is a very important part of that process. Moreover, having good mental health is essential if you want to promote healthy personal growth.

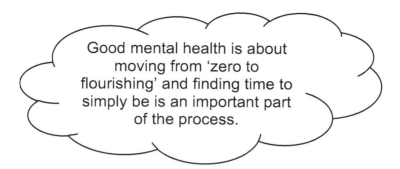

Good mental health is about moving from 'zero to flourishing' and finding time to simply be is an important part of the process.

Ego and beyond

As has been my modus operandi regularly in this book I will begin this section by looking at how 'ego' is defined before linking it to topics already covered in this chapter and earlier parts of the book.

The Longman Dictionary of Contemporary English www.ldoceonline.com defines ego as, "the opinion that you have about yourself". While www.vocabulary.com says, "your ego is your conscious mind, the part of your identity that you consider your 'self'".

Good or bad? Therefore, your ego is related to your level of confidence and belief about yourself (conscious opinion) and is "the eye through which the mind perceives reality" (Ivtzan, 2017, p. 18). Someone with a strong ego will have a real sense of who they are and be comfortable with that. The problem comes when your ego becomes too big, when your opinion about yourself is, perhaps, overrated and you may not have the skills to back up your assertions or ego reactions. Many people will immediately associate the ego with someone who is egotistical, who is self-centred, and who feels that the world revolves around them. Typically, learners that I teach will vary considerably in how much 'ego' they present, and some have a mismatch in their perceived level of ability (conscious overrating) and the reality, while others underrate themselves.

Thinking back to chapter 7, I mentioned how 'pride' is a positive emotion that follows performing with creativity and pride could certainly bolster your ego when you feel you have done a job well. But pride tends to be double edged with some people considering it to be negative and I would concur that too much pride, especially centred on oneself could easily lead to an egocentric attitude.

So, my assertion is that your ego can be expressed in good or bad ways and once again it is all about balance in the same way as being and doing require balance.

So how do you move beyond ego? Indeed, what does it mean to move beyond ego? How can you quieten your ego? And why might this be a good thing? Wow, a lot of questions to consider. Let me begin by reminding you about Figure 3, in chapter 2, which is about mapping Learning Zones onto the Diamond Model of Skill Acquisition. In this model one of the suggested by-products of flow experiences is moving beyond the ego, while another is that your self-concept is strengthened. A strong self-concept (comprised of self-esteem, self-image and ideal self; Rogers, 1959), unlike a big ego, tends to be based on reality; the reality of enhanced ability, achievement and matching challenge with skills all of which come from regularly experiencing flow. And this strengthened self-concept and belief in one's abilities dissipates the need for a big ego. In other words, you become quietly confident and the need to 'blow your own trumpet', so to speak, disappears. Therefore, flow experiences are one route to moving beyond ego or not feeling the need for ego to dominate.

Meditation and mindfulness are another route to moving beyond ego. Itai Ivtzan (2015) in his wonderful book 'Awareness is Freedom' talks about how everyone develops 'ego concepts' and how these are comprised of your beliefs, thoughts and experiences and they are often formed as a defence against challenges or when you feel threatened or vulnerable. The problem is that they become your perceived reality, habitual, even when the threat, challenge etc. is no longer present and this leads to making assumptions about, and reacting to, yourself, others, and the surrounding world. So, it is your ego concepts that come together to create your ego or self; who you believe you are and also who you believe you are not! However, your true authentic self lies beneath this masquerade of the ego and it is through meditation and mindfulness that you can firstly, bring your attention to the present moment and secondly, learn not to react to thoughts. Therefore, "non-reactive attention" (Ivtzan, 2015, p. 59) is a skill that can be developed through meditation and mindfulness practice which in turn will reduce or weaken your ego concepts thereby allowing your true authentic self to come to the fore.

As I already stated earlier, ego can be expressed in good or bad ways, but meditation and mindfulness practice increase your awareness and give you the choice of how to respond (rather than react) to the world. Your ego is how you see yourself and it is important that this *formed self-created self* is healthy so that you can have pride in your achievements, be proud of who you are and what you 'do', while at the same time being able to take time to authentically 'be'. In other words, find a healthy balance between human being and human doing.

Self-transcendence

In the last chapter, I covered the idea of self-actualisation and how it became synonymous with being the pinnacle of Maslow's hierarchy of needs. But self-transcendence or simply transcendence is seen as a further step in human growth and development where you move beyond the boundaries of the self to an understanding of your part within the bigger universe. This includes your friends, family and work networks, current and future community, organisations, generations and wider ecology. The word transcend simply means to go beyond so you can transcend many things; transcend your ego (as already discussed), transcend this world when you die and enter another (as purported by many religions), transcend your socioeconomic barriers through education etc. Indeed, Scott Barry Kaufmann (2020) talks about how Maslow himself presented many different examples of transcendence. However, in the context of this book, and the LEFG method, transcendence means growing in such a way as to move beyond just the needs of the self to wanting to help others, the wider community and the world and each person's contribution to the wider community will be different. For me it relates back to my purpose of helping others improve their health and well-being through sport and mountain life. Teachers and coaches from any domain are ideally placed to help others but probably one of the most obvious examples of helping others, in our current world, are all those health care workers who have been caring for people affected by the COVID-19 pandemic. But it is more than simply helping others (some might say that is simply human nature at its best), it is understanding how your contribution fits within the wider context of the planet – our planet.

The final part of this chapter offers some practical things you can do to increase the time that you spend being so that you can redress the balance between being and doing thereby encouraging personal growth and development and moving closer to self-actualisation and self-transcendence. After reading through *my list* of ways to be more present I invite you to create your own list.

Ten ways to simply be that I enjoy and find useful:

1. **Be with your breath** – spend anything between five to 20 minutes meditating each day. I personally find using apps like Insight Timer[53] to be excellent. There are many different forms of meditation available, allowing you to vary your practice, and find which types of meditation work best for you. You will tend to gravitate towards certain teachers and my personal favourites are Sharon Salzberg, John Siddique and Andrew Johnson. I also enjoy using the timer and just meditating without any guidance. Focusing on breathing using different anchors, body sensations and listening to sounds in the environment are all great ways to stay present moment focused. And for a really fun way to

---

[53] Insight Timer https://insighttimer.com is a FREE app for meditation aimed at relieving stress and anxiety, promoting sleep, relaxation, loving kindness and more.

pause and meditate during the day why not use the free SELFIE App[54], a concept developed by a couple of my friends and colleagues from the MAPP course. While it may be aimed more at children it is really fun and useful. Check it out to find out what the acronym SELFIE stands for!

2. **Be free from social media** or even better have a break from all electronic devices. This could be for half a day or a whole day. I use social media a lot for business as well as personal life, but it can easily creep up on you to the point that you are constantly checking your phone and going onto various social media platforms! Combine this with watching TV and your whole life can become a constant reliance on technology!

3. **Be with the sky**. I like to sit outside in the evening and watch the sky over the Chaines des Aravis (Aravis mountains) which can range from a beautiful deep blue colour contrasting the outline of the mountain range to amazing cloud formations. Just watching the sky at night can evoke a host of positive emotions such as awe and serenity and can link to the idea of self-

---

[54] Amazing Minds CIC came up with the SELFIE idea and with the help of the Positive Psychology Research Centre and Enrapture Web Design developed this free App available on Apple and Google Play.
https://apps.apple.com/gb/app/selfie-time/id1514421957

transcendence where, as an individual, you appreciate being part of something much bigger.

4. **Be in nature.** I enjoy taking short slower paced walks and just looking at everything nature has to offer, be it the new growth of spring, the summer flowers, the autumn colours or the snow-capped mountains as winter approaches. A relatively recent review of research literature by Colin Capaldi and colleagues (2015) gives support for the idea that being in nature is one route to a more flourishing life.

5. **Be with your music.** For me this means listening to relaxing music such as jazz, blues or easy listening but, ultimately, it's whatever genre you prefer so that you can immerse yourself in the music. There is clearly a link between music and mindfulness with many of the meditation Apps including guided sessions with background music. Indeed, when I did my Meditation and Mindfulness Teacher Training[55], under the excellent tutelage of Itai Ivtzan, one of the topics covered was whether we preferred having guided sessions with or without background music. Clearly it is a personal preference, but many people seem to find music to be a great way to relax and de-stress.

---

[55] The Meditation and Mindfulness Teacher Training course referred to is run by the School of Positive Transformation, and I can highly recommend it.
https://www.schoolofpositivetransformation.com/meditation-and-mindfulness-teacher-training/

6. **Be in the mountains.** I love to get out hiking in the mountains in summer and autumn and go ski touring in winter and spring. This is certainly a time to find awe and appreciate the majestic beauty whether it's the alps or the Scottish hills. The benefits of hiking are many including physical exercise, positive emotions evoked by the scenery and the mental stimulation from getting away from normal day to day life.

7. **Be with your friends.** Spend quality time with your friends and make an effort to really listen to their conversation without interrupting or trying to think of the next thing to say as they are talking.

8. **Be with your food.** Take time to eat your meals and to savour each mouthful. Try eating your dinner without watching TV – just be mindful of and appreciate your food.

9. **Be with your senses.** Just sit somewhere and listen to all the sounds around you. I like to do this in the garden but also when riding ski-lifts in winter.

10. **Be with your pets.** For me spending time with my dogs is a great way to relax and be present. Whether that's petting and cuddling them, going on walks in the mountains, or a great adventure with them in our campervan. Some research also suggests that pet owners have higher levels of

well-being than non-pet owners and a study carried out by Katherine Jacobs Bao and George Schreer (2016) suggests that owning a dog in particular is associated with well-being benefits.

PAUSE

I recommend that before reading the final chapter of this book that you stop reading and write your own list of ways to simply be (if you are reading the print version then you can use one of the 'notes, thoughts & ideas' pages at the back of the book). Make it personal and include things that you enjoy doing. The important thing is that these allow you to be in the moment, either for a short or extended period of time.

Be with your pets

CHAPTER 13

Find hope and meaning

Questions to ponder:

⇒ What is hope?
⇒ How can you find and maintain hope in challenging times?
⇒ Does finding your meaning involve others?

On Saturday the 14th of March 2020 I woke early as normal got out promptly to walk our dogs before leaving for work. I had a morning ski lesson at Le Tour one of the Chamonix valley ski domains and unusually both my wife Shona and I were teaching in the same place – more often than not we would have lessons booked in different ski areas. As we drove to work that morning the spectre of coronavirus was looming large. Italy had gone into a national 'lockdown' almost a week before and the ski areas had been progressively closing down prior to that. Some Austrian ski resorts in the Tyrol had been rife with the virus. We knew that it was just a matter of time before France followed suit. But the whole situation was incredibly hard to comprehend. It just seemed unthinkable that our winter season could come to such an abrupt end. So many thoughts were running through our heads as we both contemplated what lay ahead.

That lesson turned out to be my final one of the 2019/2020 winter season. The ski areas all closed that night and by Tuesday the 17th of March, France had also imposed a national lockdown. Just one year before we had been in Pamporovo, Bulgaria at the opening ceremony of World Interski with Team Ireland and celebrating not only the start of a great congress but also St. Patrick's Day. But the situation we now faced a year on was like something out of a science fiction movie except that we were characters in the movie and the movie was reality!

In some ways this chapter is the one that I have been looking forward to writing the most, not because it is an easy one to write, but rather because it is being written at a time in the history of humankind where hope and meaning are perhaps needed more than ever. The world is suffering the worst pandemic due to COVID-19 since the Spanish flu of 1918 and with it has come massive uncertainty, economic hardship and a whole host of other challenges and problems that are, and will continue, revealing themselves as time moves forward.

After *my office* was taken away from me in March 2020, I could not help feeling sorry for myself, or starting to worry about all the permutations of what was happening. My days were initially filled with watching the news and following everything on social media and I quickly came to realise that this was not healthy for my mind. I was reminded of the words of Zig Ziglar who said, "you are who you are and what you are because of what has gone into your mind. You can change who you are and what you are by changing what goes into your mind" (2014, p. 14). Now don't misunderstand me as I am not saying that you should simply block out what is happening in the

FIND HOPE AND MEANING

world, particularly when there is a crisis happening of the magnitude of COVID-19, but continually filling my mind relentlessly with negative and highly repetitious input was not doing me any good. So, I needed to find a balance where I could keep up to date with the reality of the situation but not overload myself with this stream of information much of which was simply conjecture about how things might unfold.

One of the surprising things about human beings is how quickly they can adjust to what might be termed a new normal. 'Social distancing'[56] was becoming part of that life moving forwards. But the first three weeks of lockdown were particularly challenging. I was, like so many others, experiencing a huge range of emotions, moving from *self-pity* to *concern* for all those people out there putting themselves at risk on the front line, to *sadness* for all those who were dying and for their loved ones who were grieving (and in many cases unable to properly grieve due to funeral restrictions). Then there was the *fear* of people you know getting the virus be it friends, family etc., and of course, the *worry* of getting it yourself. Then there was the *guilt* of knowing how much better off I was than many others; those in countries where the lockdown was even more severe, those in apartment buildings without balconies or gardens etc. COVID-19 was aggravating a plethora of other problems e.g., loneliness, depression, domestic violence,

---

[56] Social distancing is a classic example of how society can misuse language and by doing so add to the negativity and fear surrounding the pandemic. In reality the term should be 'physical distancing' as this is what is actually required while at the same time maintaining social interaction and connection. The unfortunate consequence of this term has been to add angst to people's feelings thereby negatively impacting well-being.

cancelled cancer treatments etc., and was really highlighting the inequalities of the world.

It took me three weeks before I could finally write a blog about hope (Tate, 2020c). In that time one of the things I did was to read Viktor Frankl's (2004) hugely influential book, 'Man's Search for Meaning'. I had previously read parts of the book but mainly part two, which focuses on logotherapy[57]. I had avoided part one about his experiences in a concentration camp because I felt it would be too painful to read! I was scared that I would find it to be a harrowing tale of humanity at its worst akin to my experience when I visited the House of Terror, in Budapest, in the summer of 2018. But I could not have been more wrong.

On entering 'lockdown' I decided to read the book in its entirety, and I am so glad that I did. In spite of the disgust and horror that one feels when reading the first half, about the Holocaust, Frankl had a way of writing that allows the reader to find both meaning and hope from this terrible part of human history.

Meaning from suffering is very much the message that Frankl wishes to convey but NOT that one should seek suffering – after all this is a part of life that everyone has to deal with to a greater or lesser extent. This is perhaps summed up by part of a talk Frankl gave to his fellow prisoners where he recollects saying, "human life, under

---

[57] Logotherapy is Frankl's version of psychotherapy. In essence, logotherapy focuses on the future and on having meaning in one's life so it "is a meaning-centered psychotherapy" (Frankl, 2004, p. 104).

any circumstances, never ceases to have a meaning, and that this infinite meaning of life includes suffering and dying, privation and death" (p. 90). He stressed that even in the hopelessness of their situation (just trying to remain alive each day) that they should not lose hope but rather keep their courage and their dignity.

Reading the first half of the book, not surprisingly, brings more value to the second half and a greater understanding of what logotherapy is all about. But it is the 1984 postscript, The Case for Tragic Optimism, that really impacted me because, in the current pandemic situation, the following quote really gave me a wakeup call: "If one cannot change a situation that causes his suffering, he can still choose his attitude" (p. 148). And this is so true however difficult it may seem at times. While many people are no doubt suffering and have indeed suffered (to varying degrees) due to COVID-19 how does this even begin to compare to the incredible suffering that the prisoners endured in the likes of Auschwitz, Dachau, Majdanek to name just a few? Context is everything and can certainly help to give one a kick up the back side, which I certainly needed!

What is hope?
During my first year on the MAPP course we studied 'Hope' and some of the first literature we looked at was the work of Charles Snyder and his psychological construct of hope (2002). Initially this really resonated with me because of its practical approach incorporating pathways thinking (route) and agency thinking (motivation and determination) to the achievement of goals. Coming from a sporting background where the

setting of, and working towards, gaols is such a crucial part of success this seemed, to me, to be such a logical approach. Indeed, there has been a good deal of reference to goals throughout this book ranging from short-term task or practice session goals to longer-term goals and dreams, but is this really all there is to hope?

Joanna Macy and Chris Johnstone in their excellent and thought-provoking book 'Active Hope' (2012) define hope in two ways; firstly, they talk about 'hope' in terms of being hopeful with the prospect that the things hoped for will come true. However, they point out that the problem with this kind of passive hope is that action is only likely to occur when there is a reasonably good chance of the outcome coming to fruition. The second type of hope they refer to is more active and is more emotionally driven by desire. Thinking back to chapter 5, there is certainly a great deal of overlap here with developing passion and the idea that passion is the emotional fuel needed to drive you to action towards your longer-term goals. I encourage you to take another look at Figure 7 as you will see that you could easily replace the word passion with the words active hope and the model would work perfectly in terms of active hope creating the desire (emotional fuel) necessary to move along the pathway towards longer-term goal achievement.

In relation to what I have presented in this book I would say that 'active hope' involves 'doing' but doing that is based on responding NOT reacting and this necessitates a period of 'being' mindful before deciding your intention. When I train ski instructors one of the things that I always stress about giving feedback on their learner's performance, after they have observed it, is that they should; pause, ask, tell (a well-known acronym PAT). In

FIND HOPE AND MEANING

other words, pause, and reflect on what they have observed, so that they can respond with a question to the learner about their performance, and then follow that up with telling them only what they need to (after listening to the learner's response). Therefore, a similar considered approach to 'active hope' (or lasting hope as I like to call it) could be; pause, be, decide, do. **Pause** and reflect on what has happened (past), **be** present with your current situation, **decide** on your intention and what needs to be done (future) and then **do** (take action). This process ensures that hope for the future is based on the past and present and is consequently more likely to inspire action that can withstand the setbacks that will undoubtedly occur. Hence lasting hope is grounded in reality.

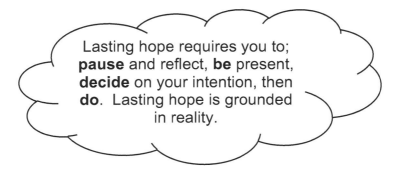

Lasting hope requires you to; **pause** and reflect, **be** present, **decide** on your intention, then **do**. Lasting hope is grounded in reality.

Hope vs. optimism

The terms hope and optimism, hopeful, optimistic etc. often get used interchangeably yet researchers generally see these concepts as quite different and do not necessarily agree on their definitions! Based on the earlier discussion I see hope as something that you work towards, something that is future oriented while optimism can help you get there.

In the same way as Zig Ziglar (1997) says that failure is related to the event (not the person) and is therefore transitory and event related (mentioned way back in chapter 1), Martin Seligman (2006) in his book 'Learned Optimism' talks about "the art of hope" (p. 48) being about seeing adversity and bad luck as being temporary and specific. In other words, if you can find reasons for your misfortune that suggest it is just a temporary setback, and specific to that one event, then you are much more likely to be hopeful. Conversely, if you tend to explain such events as being permanent and not specific to that one situation then you lose hope. And Seligman's optimism test, from the book just mentioned, is based on how people explain events with 'hope' being an integral part of that test to see how much optimism you have.

The chicken and egg scenario once again comes to the fore because the suggestion is that hope breeds optimism, but equally it could hold true that optimistic people are more hopeful!

Angela Duckworth (2016) sees hope as being one of the four psychological assets that are needed for developing grit (the others being interest, practice and purpose). She says that the kind of hope required for grit is one based on effort being the key to improving the future and not just wishful thinking. Hence that kind of gritty hope will lead to being more optimistic. This would appear to support the idea that having hope leads to being more optimistic.

Snyder (2002) posits that hope theory is different to optimism in that the agency and pathways thinking leads to future positive goal related outcomes and that there is greater emphasis on the outcome in hope theory.

In an attempt to conclude this debate, I would say that hope can be seen, quite coldly, as an outcome or goal (more akin to Snyder's hope theory). But, in reality, it is also wrapped up in emotion (hopeful) and your attitude (the way you explain circumstances). It can also be active (positive) or passive (wishful). Optimism is about responding to challenges with confidence and a belief that the future will be better. But as Simon Sinek[58] says optimism is not naïve, or the denial of reality, which correlates with the earlier emphasis about hope suggesting that both (hope and optimism) are grounded in reality. So, being realistic appears to be an important part of creating lasting hope and this in turn breeds optimism. In these current times, with the coronavirus pandemic presenting all sorts of challenges, it is vital for hope and optimism to be based on reality while being 'open' to seeing opportunities that present themselves and alternative pathways to reaching your goals. Surely this kind of mature approach is a sign of growth?

Maintaining hope
Losing hope: I can almost hear you (the reader) saying, but what happens when hope is lost? What happens when life's challenges pile up and things become

---

[58] Simon Sinek is a motivational speaker and author with many YouTube videos. Near the beginning of the COVID-19 lockdown he released a short video about optimism and how it is not naïve like positivity https://youtu.be/roDLXM70du0

overwhelming? Simply being told to adopt a positive attitude, or explain things in temporary and specific ways, is all well and good but remaining actively hopeful and optimistic may not be easy and that is where resilience becomes important.

Resilience: This is another of these words (like mindfulness) that has become a modern buzzword and gets overused! However, it is an important part of positive psychology and vital for dealing with, and bouncing back from, the more challenging and troubling times in your life and therefore works hand in hand with hope in that someone who is very resilient will be better able to maintain or re-establish hope.

Resilience is about mental toughness and how quickly you can recover from setbacks, injury, illness and how quickly you can adapt to change. Karen Reivich and Andrew Shatte (2002) define it very simply as, "the ability to persevere and adapt when things go awry" (p. 1).

What kind of things have you encountered recently that have stressed you and required resilience? Perhaps there have been challenges at work – too much to do, awkward colleagues, demanding boss. Challenges at home – too many bills, arguments with your spouse, noisy children etc. Or challenges relating to sport – not enough time to get out there and practice, injuries, poor results. The challenges can be many and if you add in COVID-19 lockdown and restrictions suddenly these stressors take on a whole new level.

There is no doubt that everyone needs resilience and you probably know some people that you consider to be resilient. All of the contributors to this book have shown great resilience, at various stages through their lives, and I say that from knowing them (some better than others of course). They serve as role models to others and none more so than David Smith whom I introduced back in chapter 6. If you have forgotten David's story, then take a moment to refresh your memory and you will see that David has had more challenges and adversity than most people you will ever meet and yet is one of the most resilient people I have ever come across. So, putting things in perspective can in itself be useful but how can you increase your resilience? Is it possible to become more resilient? The answer is YES and like so many things covered in this book the answer lies in purposeful practice. But what is it that you need to practice and do?

While there is a great deal of good advice available on how to improve your resilience it would seem appropriate to relate the improvement of resilience to the wealth of content that is contained in the pages that you have read in this book and with that in mind I have come up with an easy to remember acronym for improving resilience which is **ACT**: Actions, Character strengths and Thoughts.

Actions: - is about doing and performing which means learning new skills, challenging yourself, failing and being allowed to fail, experiencing flow, building self-confidence, discovering your purpose and helping others.

Character strengths: - means discovering and using your strengths, both character and skills, thus increasing enjoyment and engagement in what you do, which in turn will develop a sense of control and competence.

Thoughts: - means practicing meditation and mindfulness, including mindful learning, so that you can better control your thoughts. The overriding intention of the practice is to learn to respond rather than react.

Hopefully by reading the short descriptions for ACT it will remind you that all of these things have been covered, in some detail, in the previous chapters and there are many references and footnotes provided so that you can delve more deeply into any specific areas that are of particular interest. In essence by following the LEFG coaching method you will build your resilience and if you feel your resilience needs a boost remember to ACT. This will help you to more easily maintain hope even when the going gets tough. But there is one more important aspect of hope to discuss…

The gift of hope

While maintaining hope is a constant challenge for the *individual* one of the best ways to improve your own well-being is in the service of others and, to this end, hope is one of the greatest gifts that you can give to another person because it encourages them and moves them towards their goals. Zig Ziglar, one of my favourite motivational speakers of all time, was very much an encourager and someone who gave many people around the world hope. In his final book, 'Born to Win' he said, "encouragement and hope are critical to success" (2014, p. 95). So being an encourager and giver of hope is a laudable quality for anyone and if you are a coach, or teacher, it is something to aspire to be with as many of your learners as possible and if it is part of your purpose then even better. What a great example of transcending the self and growing.

Understanding meaning

Whether hope precedes meaning or meaning provides hope is another of those questions that is difficult to answer. What is more important to establish here though is that I am talking about 'meaning in life' and not, the bigger philosophical question about, the 'meaning of life'. Meaning in life can be very much seen as part of the process of growing (individually and collectively) and from continually engaging with the learn, enjoy, flow and grow coaching method. So, perhaps, lasting hope and true meaning sit side by side and are both the products of self-actualisation hence my reasoning for including these two very important aspects of human life in the same chapter at the end of this book.

Michael Steger (2012) says that there are two aspects to meaning with the first being about understanding your life, making sense of the world in which you live and the lens through which you view it. The second aspect is purpose, which he says is about having "one or more overarching, long-term life aspirations" (p. 382). Interestingly, as pointed out in chapter 11, discovering your purpose takes time as you make sense of your life! It is hardly surprising then that the terms meaning, and purpose are often interchanged being seen as similar by researchers in the field a point alluded to by Steger himself. Therefore, my assertion would be, that sense making in life (one part of meaning) is required in order to discover your purpose and by achieving the latter you find true meaning.

Emily Esfahani Smith (2017) breaks meaning down further suggesting that there are "four pillars of meaning: belonging, purpose, storytelling, and transcendence" (p. 41). This certainly relates to Steger's definition above in that 'purpose' forms one of the pillars, and 'storytelling' (see McAdams, 1993) correlates with sense making. While her fourth pillar: 'transcendence' (see Kaufmann, 2020) has been covered in the preceding chapter. That leaves 'belonging' which Smith emphasises is about finding meaning through others, and with others, rather than it being an individual journey.

Meaning and positive psychology

Given that the content of this book is underpinned by the principles of positive psychology (PP) how does PP fit with, or contribute to, meaning in life and growth both of the individual and society?

Before the first wave of PP, 'psychology' was primarily focused on illness and dysfunction and on fixing what was wrong. First wave PP concentrated on studying the 'positive' aspects of well-being, and on improving what was right, with happiness as a strong outcome focus (Seligman & Csikszentmihalyi, 2000). Second wave PP built on this by incorporating the 'negative' and how a greater understanding of the interplay between positive and negative could lead to better well-being (Ivtzan, Lomas, Hefferon, & Worth, 2016). This development of PP was prompted and assisted by the contributions of existential psychologist and meaning-centred researcher

Dr. Paul Wong[59] (2011a, 2011b). And now third wave PP proposes that PP broadens its well-being focus to move beyond the individual and incorporate the study of different groups, systems, cultures etc. thus redressing the balance from 'Western' cultures, where PP originated, to incorporate a worldwide view that recognises these differences (Lomas, Waters, Williams, Oades, & Kern, 2020). This broadening of research focus would appear to fit well with the idea of transcendence beyond the self (Kaufmann, 2020) and moving beyond the ego (Ivtzan, 2015) creating conditions conducive for making meaning in life (Steger, 2012).

It seems only fitting that the final quote of this book, in a chapter on hope and meaning, should be from Viktor Frankl who's accounts of finding hope and meaning in the most desperate of circumstances are a lesson to everyone:

> "Life ultimately means taking the responsibility to find the right answer to its problems and to fulfil the tasks which it constantly sets for each individual" (2004, p. 85).

---

[59] Dr Paul Wong's contribution to the fields of existential psychology, meaning and positive psychology have been huge. He is the founder and president of the International Network on Personal Meaning https://www.meaning.ca

If you take just one message from this book, then it is to RESPOND to life rather than react.

Mindful alpine scenery

EPILOUGE

Bringing it all together

Now that you have read this entire book and grasped how each part of the LEFG method works this short conclusion aims to bring everything together. On a number of occasions (including right back in the introduction), I have emphasised that the *method* is cyclical, and you can move clockwise or anti clockwise with the crucial understanding that each *part* impacts the other or others. The final model of this book, Figure 12, presents a four-quadrant model of the Learn, Enjoy, Flow and Grow method.

Each of the four quadrants contains the ideal in terms of what you should be aiming for in order to maximise this part of the method, whether it is a self-coaching method, or a method you, as a coach, use with your learners. In other words;

- What should you/the learner be experiencing?
- What are the beliefs associated with these experiences?
- What are the key questions?
- What are the main benefits to be derived?

So, beginning top right with **learn** the goal is to do this in a way that creates enjoyment. However, this can also contribute to your growth.

Four 'parts' that lead to a better life

GROW (4)
I am life & life is me

Experience: Transcendence
Moving beyond ego

Beliefs: Growth is a result of the previous three
Growth is a worthwhile pursuit

Question: Being or doing?

Benefits: Enhances learning
Self-actualisation
Loss of ego
Contentment
Hope and meaning

LEARN (1)
I am curious & open minded

Experience: Interest, challenge, curiosity

Beliefs: Learning involves failure
Practice must be purposeful
Skill maximises talent

Questions: What am I interested in?
What do I want to learn?

Benefits: Discover your strengths
Develop new skills
BEE Focused
Become more mindful

FLOW (3)
I flow with mindfulness

Experience: Effortless attention
Action-awareness merging
Sense of control
Loss of self consciousness
Transformation of time

Beliefs: The foundations are controllable
Worth doing for its own sake

Question: Can I make flow happen?

Benefits: Pleasure derived post activity
Wanting more of the same
Accelerates learning

ENJOY (2)
I am intrinsically motivated

Experience: Excitement, fun, joy

Beliefs: Passion is the fuel that drives you forwards
The journey is more important than the destination

Questions: What are my internal drivers?
Am I flexible with my goals?

Benefits: Pleasure, satisfaction
Increased motivation
Being more creative
Realising goals and dreams

This model is cyclical and works both clockwise and anti clockwise.

© Derek Tate 2020

Figure 12.

When you **enjoy** the process/journey you enhance your learning. Learn and enjoy combine to encourage flow.

And **flow** experiences promote growth. But one of the most important by-products of experiencing flow is enjoyment. While being in flow can also accelerate the learning process.

And as you **grow** you learn more and create a mental state that is more conducive to finding flow.

The beauty of this model is the interaction between the four parts which are all equally important (even though I previously said that 'flow' could be considered the holy grail, but this is only because it can seem elusive).

Whatever you learn in life, and no matter what the domain, this method can be applied and by doing so you can live a much fuller life and one that is filled with passion and meaning.

I wish you well on all the journeys still to come.

REFERENCES

Introduction

Ivtzan, I., Lomas, T., Hefferon, K., & Worth, P. (2016). *Second wave positive psychology : embracing the dark side of life*. London and New York: Routledge.

Kaufman, S. B. (2020). *Transcend: The science of self-actualization*. TarcherPerigee.

Maslow, A. H. (1943). A theory of human motivation. *Psychological Review*, 370–396.

Seligman, M. E. P., & Csikszentmihalyi, M. (2000). Positive psychology: An introduction. *American Psychologist*, 55(1), 5–14. https://doi.org/10.1037/0003-066X.55.1.5

Tate, D. (2015). *Learn it, love it, live it: The philosophy of the Irish Association of Snowsports Instructors*. Parallel Dreams Publishing. Retrieved from https://itunes.apple.com/us/book/learn-it-love-it-live-it/id1030691073?mt=11

Chapter 1

Campbell, J., & Moyers, B. D. (1988). *The power of myth*. Doubleday.

Duckworth, A. (2016). *Grit : the power of passion and perseverance*. London: Vermilion.

Dweck, C. S. (2012). *Mindset: Changing the way you think to fulfil your potential*. Robinson.

Epstein, D. (2019). *Range : How generalists triumph in a specialized world*. Macmillan.

Fredrickson, B. L. (2010). *Positivity : groundbreaking research to release your inner optimist and thrive*. Oneworld.

Gladwell, M. (2009). *Outliers : the story of success*. Penguin Books.

Linley, A. (2008). *Average to A+ : Realising strengths in yourself and others*. Coventry: CAPP Press.

Linley, A., & Bateman, T. (2018). *The strengths profile book: Finding what you can do + love to do and why it matters* (2nd ed.). CAPP Press.

Syed, M. (2011). *Bounce : The myth of talent and the power of practice*. London: Fourth Estate.

Wapnick, E. (2015). Why some of us don't have one true calling | TED Talk. Retrieved from https://www.ted.com/talks/emilie_wapnick_why_some_of_us_don_t_have_one_true_calling

Ziglar, Z. (1997). *Over the top: Moving from survival to stability, from stability to success, from success to significance* (Revised). Nashville, Atlanta, London, Vancouver: Thomas Nelson Publishers.

Chapter 2

Coyle, D. (2009). *The talent code: Greatness isn't born, it's grown. Here's how*. Bantam Books.

Csikszentmihalyi, M. (1975). *Beyond boredom and anxiety*. Jossey-Bass Publishers.

Csikszentmihalyi, M. (1990). *Flow: The psychology of optimal experience*. New York: HarperCollins.

Csikszentmihalyi, M. (1997b). *Finding flow : The psychology of engagement with everyday life*. New York: BasicBooks.

Doran, G. T. (1981). There's a S.M.A.R.T way to write management's goals and objectives. *Management Review, 70*(11), 35–36.

Ericsson, K. A., Krampe, R. T., & Tesch-Romer, C. (1993). The Role of deliberate practice in the acquisition of expert performance. *Psychological Review, 100*(3), 363–406. https://doi.org/10.1037/0033-295x.100.3.363

Ericsson, K. A., & Pool, R. (2016). *Peak : secrets from the new science of expertise*. London: The Bodley Head.

REFERENCES

Fitts, P. M., & Posner, M. I. (1967). *Human performance.* Brooks/Cole Publishers.

Gladwell, M. (2009). *Outliers : the story of success.* Penguin Books.

Jackson, S. A., & Csikszentmihalyi, M. (1999). *Flow in sports: The keys to optimal experiences and performances.* Human Kinetics.

Kaufman, S. B. (2013). *Ungifted : intelligence redefined.* New York: Basic Books.

Langer, E. J. (1998). *The power of mindful learning.* Cambridge: Perseus Books.

Langer, E. J. (2000). Mindful learning. *Current Directions in Psychological Science, 9*(6), 220–223. https://doi.org/10.1111/1467-8721.00099

Lee, B. (2016). *Striking thoughts : Bruce Lee's wisdom for daily living.* (J. R. Little, Ed.). Tokyo, Rutland and Singapore: Tuttle Pub.

Lockerbie, A., & Tate, D. (2012). *Ski instructors handbook: teaching tools and techniques.* Parallel Dreams Publishing.

Macnamara, B. N., Hambrick, D. Z., & Oswald, F. L. (2014). Deliberate practice and performance in music, games, sports, education, and professions a meta-analysis. *Psychological Science, 25*(8), 1608–1618.

Monney, H. (2010). *The science of skiing: The art of performance* (First). BASS Productions.

Mosston, M., & Ashworth, S. (2002). *Teaching physical education* (Fifth edit). B. Cummings.

Syed, M. (2011). *Bounce : The myth of talent and the power of practice.* London: Fourth Estate.

Tate, D. (2017b, July). Lesson 2: Purposeful practice. *Flowing with Mindfulness,* 1–5. Retrieved from https://www.flowingwithmindfulness.com/articles

Tate, D. (2018a). The diamond model of skill acquisition. In *Irish Association of Snowsports Instructors Manual: The four key concepts.* Irish Association of Snowsports Instructors.

Tate, D. (2018b, June). Developing your skill with mindfulness and flow: The new diamond model of skill acquisition. *Flowing with Mindfulness*, 1–5.

Tate, D. (2019b). Learning zones - part 1: From preparation to flow. Retrieved from https://www.paralleldreams.co.uk/post/learning-zones-part-1

Tate, D. (2019c). Learning zones - part 2: Mapping learning zones onto the diamond model of skill acquisition. Retrieved from https://www.paralleldreams.co.uk/post/learning-zones-part-2

Tate, D., & Kagan, J. (2018). The IASI Skills Model (SM). In *Irish Association of Snowsports Instructors Manual: The four key concepts*. Irish Association of Snowsports Instructors.

Wilson, L., & Wilson, H. (1998). *Play to win!: choosing growth over fear in work and life*. (L. Stephen, Ed.) (First). Austin: Bard Press.

Chapter 3

Cathcart, S., McGregor, M., & Groundwater, E. (2014). Mindfulness and flow in elite athletes. *Journal of Clinical Sport Psychology*, 8(2), 119–141. https://doi.org/10.1123/jcsp.2014-0018

Csikszentmihalyi, M. (2002). *Flow: The classic work on how to achieve happiness*. Rider.

Dietrich, A., & Stoll, O. (2010). Effortless attention, hypofrontality, and perfectionism. In B. Bruya (Ed.), *Effortless attention: A new perspective in the cognitive science of attention and action* (pp. 159–178). Cambridge and London: The MIT Press. https://doi.org/10.7551/mitpress/9780262013840.003.0008

REFERENCES

Ivtzan, I., & Lomas, T. (Eds.). (2016). *Mindfulness in positive psychology: The science of meditation and wellbeing.* London and New York: Routledge.

Kaufman, S. B., & Gregoire, C. (2016). *Wired to create: unraveling the mysteries of the creative mind.* TarcherPerigee.

Killingsworth, M. A., & Gilbert, D. T. (2010). A wandering mind is an unhappy mind. *Science, 330*(6006), 932. https://doi.org/10.1126/science.1192439

Moran, A. P. (1996). *The psychology of concentration in sport performers: a cognitive analysis.* Psychology Press.

Schooler, J. W., Mrazek, M. D., Franklin, M. S., Baird, B., Mooneyham, B. W., Zedelius, C., & Broadway, J. M. (2014). The middle way: Finding the balance between mindfulness and mind-wandering. In B. H. Ross (Ed.), *The psychology of learning and motivation volume 60* (pp. 1–33). Elsevier.

Shafir, R. Z. (2003). *The Zen of listening: mindful communication in the age of distraction* (2nd ed.). Wheaton and Chennai: Quest Books.

Tate, D. (2017a, June). Lesson 1 - Focus your attention. *Flowing with Mindfulness,* 1–4. Retrieved from https://www.flowingwithmindfulness.com/articles

Tate, D. (2019a). Focus of attention in sport: Internal or external? Retrieved from https://www.paralleldreams.co.uk/post/focus-of-attention-in-sport-internal-or-external

Tate, D. (2019d). *Mindful ascending for flowing descending: Can teaching alpine ski instructors mindfulness strategies foster more flow experiences on the slopes?* Buckinghamshire New University.

Wulf, G., & Lewthwaite, R. (2010). Effortless motor learning?: An external focus of attention enhances movement effectiveness and efficiency. In B. Bruya (Ed.), *Effortless attention: A new perspective in the cognitive science of attention and action* (pp. 75–101). Cambridge and London: The MIT Press.

REFERENCES

Chapter 4

Arnold, J. (2013). *Mindful learning in sport: A dissertation presented in partial fulfilment of the requirements for the degree of MSc in Mindfulness Studies at the University of Aberdeen.* University of Aberdeen.

Baltzell, A., Caraballo, N., Chipman, K., & Hayden, L. (2014). A qualitative study of the mindfulness meditation training for sport: Division i female soccer players??? experience. *Journal of Clinical Sport Psychology.* https://doi.org/10.1123/jcsp.2014-0030

Baltzell, A., & Summers, J. (2017). *The power of mindfulness : Mindfulness meditation training in sport (MMTS).* Springer International Publishing.

Beckers, I. (2020). Mindfulness is more than the hype. Retrieved from https://www.thepositivepsychologypeople.com/mindfulness-is-more-than-hype/

Ivtzan, I., & Hart, R. (2016). Mindfulness scholarship and interventions: A review. In A. L. Baltzell (Ed.), *Mindfulness and performance* (pp. 3–28). Boston: Cambridge University Press.

Ivtzan, I., & Lomas, T. (Eds.). (2016). *Mindfulness in positive psychology: The science of meditation and wellbeing.* London and New York: Routledge.

Ivtzan, I., & Russo-Netzer, P. (n.d.). Video session 3: Deepening your sense of mindfulness. Retrieved August 10, 2018, from https://www.schoolofpositivetransformation.com/mindfulness-based-meaning-program/

Kabat-Zinn, J. (1994). *Wherever you go, there you are: Mindfulness meditation for everyday life.* London: Piatkus.

Kaufman, S. B. (2020). *Transcend: The science of self-actualization.* TarcherPerigee.

Langer, E. J. (1997). *The power of mindful learning.* Cambridge: Perseus Books.

Langer, E. J. (2000). Mindful learning. *Current Directions in Psychological Science, 9*(6), 220–223.

Lockerbie, A., & Tate, D. (2012). *Ski instructors handbook: teaching tools and techniques.* Parallel Dreams Publishing.

Mumford, G. (2016). *The mindful athlete : secrets to pure performance.* Parallax Press.

Saltzman, A. (2018). *A still quiet place for athletes : mindfulness skills for achieving peak performance & finding flow in sports & life.* New Harbinger Publications, Inc.

Tate, D. (2020b). Function or form? What is the best approach to learning a sport? Retrieved from https://www.paralleldreams.co.uk/post/function-or-form

Chapter 5

Csikszentmihalyi, M., Latter, P., & Duranso, C. W. (2017). *Running flow: Mental immersion techniques for better running.* Human Kinetics.

Deci, E. L., Koestner, R., & Ryan, R. M. (1999). A aeta-analytic review of experiments examining the effects of extrinsic rewards on intrinsic motivation. *Psychological Bulletin, 125*(6), 627–668.

Deci, E. L., & Ryan, R. M. (1985). *Intrinsic motivation and self-determination in human behavior.* New York: Plenum.

Duckworth, A. (2016). *Grit : the power of passion and perseverance.* London: Vermilion.

Duckworth, A. L., Peterson, C., Matthews, M. D., & Kelly, D. R. (2007). Grit: Perseverance and passion for long-term goals. *Journal of Personality and Social Psychology, 92*(6), 1087–1101. https://doi.org/10.1037/0022-3514.92.6.1087

Linley, A., & Bateman, T. (2018). *The strengths profile book: Finding what you can do + love to do and why it matters* (2nd ed.). CAPP Press.

Loehr, J. E. (1986). *Mental toughness training for sports : Achieving athletic excellence*. The Stephen Greene Press, Inc.

Ryan, R. M., & Deci, E. L. (2000). Self-determination theory and the facilitation of intrinsic motivation, social development, and well-being. *American Psychologist, 55*(1), 68–78.

Ziglar, Z. (1997). *Over the top: Moving from survival to stability, from stability to success, from success to significance* (Revised). Nashville, Atlanta, London, Vancouver: Thomas Nelson Publishers.

Chapter 6

Baker, P. (1997). *Secrets of super achievers*. The Catalyst Group.

Bryant, F. B., & Veroff, J. (1984). Dimensions of subjective mental health in American men and women. *Journal of Health and Social Behavior, 25*(2), 116–135. https://doi.org/10.2307/2136664

Bryant, F. B., & Veroff, J. (2012). *Savoring: A new model od positive experience*. New York and London: Psychology Press.

Grant, H., & Dweck, C. S. (2003). Clarifying Achievement Goals and Their Impact. *Journal of Personality and Social Psychology, 85*(3), 541–553. https://doi.org/10.1037/0022-3514.85.3.541

Fredrickson, B. L. (2001). The role of positive emotions in positive psychology. The broaden-and-build theory of positive emotions. *The American Psychologist, 56*(3), 218–226. https://doi.org/10.1037/0003-066X.56.3.218

Kashdan, T. B., & Biswas-Diener, R. (2015). *The power of negative emotion : How anger, guilt and self doubt are essential to success and fulfillment.* Oneworld.

Lomas, T. (2016). The dialectics of emotion. In *Second wave positive psychology : embracing the dark side of life* (pp. 5–30). London and New York: Routledge.

Lyubomirsky, S. (2010). *The how of happiness: A practical approach to getting the life you want.* Piatkus.

Peterson, C., & Seligman, M. E. P. (2004). *Character strengths and virtues: A handbook and classification.* American Psychological Association and Oxford University Press.

Seligman, M. E. P. (2003). *Authentic happiness: Using the new positive psychology to realize your potential for lasting fulfillment.* London: Nicholas Brealey Publishing.

Chapter 7

Catmull, E. (2014). *Creativity, Inc.: Overcoming the unseen forces that stand in the way of true inspiration.* Transworld Publishers.

Cseh, G. M. (2016). Flow in creativity: A review of potential theoretical conflict. In L. Harmat, F. Orsted Andersen, F. Ullen, J. Wright, & G. Sadlo (Eds.), *Flow experience: Empirical research and applications* (p. 395). Springer International Publishing Switzerland.

Csikszentmihalyi, M. (1997a). *Creativity : The psychology of discovery and invention.* Harper Perennial.

Fredrickson, B. L. (2001). The role of positive emotions in positive psychology. The broaden-and-build theory of positive emotions. *The American Psychologist, 56*(3), 218–226. https://doi.org/10.1037/0003-066X.56.3.218

Fredrickson, B. L. (2010). *Positivity : groundbreaking research to release your inner optimist and thrive.* Oneworld.

Joffe, P. (n.d.). Creativity and decision making in sport: Build a house that can withstand any storm. Retrieved from https://www.sportsciencesupport.com/creativity-decision-making-sport-build-house-can-withstand-storm/

Kaufman, S. B., & Gregoire, C. (2016). *Wired to create : unraveling the mysteries of the creative mind*. TarcherPerigee.

McGonigal, K. (2019). *The joy of movement: How exercise helps us find happiness, hope, connection and courage*. New York: Avery.

Memmert, D. (2011). Creativity, expertise, and attention: Exploring their development and their relationships. *Article in Journal of Sports Sciences*, 29(1), 93–102. https://doi.org/10.1080/02640414.2010.528014

Moran, A. P. (1996). *The psychology of concentration in sport performers : a cognitive analysis*. Psychology Press.

Mosston, M., & Ashworth, S. (2002). *Teaching physical education* (Fifth edit). B. Cummings.

Tate, D. (2007). *Parallel dreams alpine skiing: Taking your skiing performance to new levels* (First). Parallel Dreams Publishing.

Chapter 8

Cox, R. H. (1998). *Sports psychology: Concepts and applications* (Fourth). McGraw-Hill Pub. Co.

Cseh, G. M. (2016). Flow in creativity: A review of potential theoretical conflict. In L. Harmat, F. Orsted Andersen, F. Ullen, J. Wright, & G. Sadlo (Eds.), *Flow experience: Empirical research and applications* (p. 395). Springer International Publishing Switzerland

Csikszentmihalyi, M. (1975). *Beyond boredom and anxiety*. Jossey-Bass Publishers.

Csikszentmihalyi, M. (1990). *Flow: The psychology of optimal experience*. New York: HarperCollins.

REFERENCES

Csikszentmihalyi, M. (1993). *The evolving self : A psychology for the third millennium*. HarperCollins Publishers.

Csikszentmihalyi, M. (1997b). *Finding flow : The psychology of engagement with everyday life*. New York: BasicBooks.

Csikszentmihalyi, M. (2002). *Flow: The classic work on how to achieve happiness*. Rider.

Csikszentmihalyi, M., & Larson, R. (2014). Validity and reliability of the experience-sampling method. In *Flow and the foundations of positive psychology: The collected works of Mihaly Csikszentmihalyi* (pp. 35–54). Springer Netherlands. https://doi.org/10.1007/978-94-017-9088-8_3

Csikszentmihalyi, M., Latter, P., & Duranso, C. W. (2017). *Running flow: Mental immersion techniques for better running*. Human Kinetics.

Jackson, S. A. (1992). Athletes in flow: A qualitative investigation of flow states in elite figure skaters. *Journal of Applied Sport Psychology, 4*(2), 161–180. https://doi.org/10.1080/10413209208406459

Jackson, S. A., & Csikszentmihalyi, M. (1999). *Flow in sports: The keys to optimal experiences and performances*. Human Kinetics.

Jackson, S. A., & Eklund, R. (2002). Assessing flow in physical activity: The Flow State Scale-2 and Dispositional Flow Scale-2. *Journal of Sport & Exercise Psychology, 24*(2), 133–150. https://doi.org/10.1123/jsep.24.2.133

Kotler, S. (2015). *The rise of superman : decoding the science of ultimate human performance*. Quercus Editions Ltd.

Lockerbie, A., & Tate, D. (2012). *Ski instructors handbook: teaching tools and techniques*. Parallel Dreams Publishing.

Mosston, M., & Ashworth, S. (2002). *Teaching physical education* (Fifth edit). B. Cummings.

Mumford, G. (2016). *The mindful athlete : secrets to pure performance*. Parallax Press.

Saltzman, A. (2018). *A still quiet place for athletes: mindfulness skills for achieving peak performance & finding flow in sports & life*. New Harbinger Publications, Inc.

Swann, C. (2016). Flow in sport. In L. Harmat, F. Orsted Andersen, F. Ullen, J. Wright, & G. Sadlo (Eds.), *Flow experience: Empirical research and applications* (pp. 51–64). Springer International Publishing Switzerland. https://doi.org/10.1007/978-3-319-28634-1_1

Swann, C., Crust, L., Keegan, R., Piggott, D., & Hemmings, B. (2015). An inductive exploration into the flow experiences of European Tour golfers. *Qualitative Research in Sport, Exercise and Health*, 7(2), 210–234. https://doi.org/10.1080/2159676X.2014.926969

Tate, D. (2018b, June). Developing your skill with mindfulness and flow: The new diamond model of skill acquisition. *Flowing with Mindfulness*, 1–5. Retrieved from https://www.flowingwithmindfulness.com/articles

Tate, D. (2019d). *Mindful ascending for flowing descending: Can teaching alpine ski instructors mindfulness strategies foster more flow experiences on the slopes?* Buckinghamshire New University.

Tate, D. (2020a). Facilitating flow: How the foundations interact during task performance. Retrieved from https://www.paralleldreams.co.uk/post/facilitating-flow

Ulrich, M., Keller, J., & Grö, G. (2016). Neural signatures of experimentally induced flow experiences identified in a typical fMRI block design with BOLD imaging. *Social Cognitive and Affective Neuroscience*, 11(3), 496–507. https://doi.org/10.1093/scan/nsv133

Chapter 9

Csikszentmihalyi, M. (1990). *Flow: The psychology of optimal experience*. New York: HarperCollins.

Csikszentmihalyi, M. (1993). *The evolving self : A psychology for the third millennium*. HarperCollins Publishers.

Csikszentmihalyi, M. (1997a). *Creativity : The psychology of discovery and invention*. Harper Perennial.

Csikszentmihalyi, M. (1997b). *Finding flow : The psychology of engagement with everyday life*. New York: BasicBooks.

Csikszentmihalyi, M. (2004). *Good business : Leadership, flow and the making of meaning*. Hodder & Stoughton.

Csikszentmihalyi, M., Latter, P., & Duranso, C. W. (2017). *Running flow: Mental immersion techniques for better running*. Human Kinetics.

Jackson, S. A., & Csikszentmihalyi, M. (1999). *Flow in sports: The keys to optimal experiences and performances*. Human Kinetics.

Tate, D. (2019d). *Mindful ascending for flowing descending: Can teaching alpine ski instructors mindfulness strategies foster more flow experiences on the slopes?* Buckingshire New University.

Chapter 10

Aherne, C., Moran, A. P., & Lonsdale, C. (2011). The effect of mindfulness training on athletes' flow: An initial investigation. *The Sport Psychologist*, 25(2), 177–189. https://doi.org/10.1123/tsp.25.2.177

Baltzell, A., & Summers, J. (2017). *The power of mindfulness : Mindfulness meditation training in sport (MMTS)*. Springer International Publishing.

Carron, A. V., Colman, M. M., Wheeler, J., & Stevens, D. (2002). Cohesion and performance in sport: A meta analysis. *Journal of Sport and Exercise Psychology*, 24(2), 168–188.

Cathcart, S., McGregor, M., & Groundwater, E. (2014). Mindfulness and flow in elite athletes. *Journal of Clinical Sport Psychology*, *8*(2), 119–141. https://doi.org/10.1123/jcsp.2014-0018

Cox, R. H. (1998). *Sports psychology: Concepts and applications* (Fourth). McGraw-Hill Pub. Co.

Ericsson, K. A., & Pool, R. (2016). *Peak : secrets from the new science of expertise*. London: The Bodley Head.

Frankl, V. E. (2004). *Man's search for meaning : the classic tribute to hope from the Holocaust*. Rider.

Frankl, V. E. (2012). *The doctor and the soul: From psychotherapy to logotherapy*. Souvenir Press.

Frankl, V. E. (2014). *The will to meaning: Foundations and applications of logotherapy*. Plume.

Fredrickson, B. L. (2001). The role of positive emotions in positive psychology. The broaden-and-build theory of positive emotions. *The American Psychologist*, *56*(3), 218–226. https://doi.org/10.1037/0003-066X.56.3.218

Hout, J. J. J. van den, Davis, O. C., & Walrave, B. (2016). The application of team flow theory. In László Harmat, F. Ørsted Andersen, F. Ullén, J. Wright, & G. Saldo (Eds.), *Flow experience: Empirical research and applications* (pp. 233–247). Springer International Publishing Switzerland.

Ivtzan, I. (2015). *Awareness is freedom: The adventure of psychology and spirituality.* Winchester and Washington: Changemakers Books.

Jackson, S. A. (2016a). Flow and mindfulness in performance. In A. L. Baltzell (Ed.), *Mindfulness and performance: Current perspectives in social and behavioral sciences* (pp. 78–100). Boston: Cambridge University Press.

Jackson, S. A. (2016b). Flowing with mindfulness: Investigating the relationship between flow and mindfulness. In I. Ivtzan & T. Lomas (Eds.), *Mindfulness in positive psychology : The science of meditation and wellbeing* (pp. 141–155). London and New York: Routledge.

REFERENCES

Kahneman, D. (2012). *Thinking, fast and slow*. Penguin Books.

Kashdan, T. B., & Biswas-Diener, R. (2015). *The power of negative emotion : How anger, guilt and self doubt are essential to success and fulfillment*. Oneworld.

Kaufman, K. A., Glass, C. R., & Arnkoff, D. B. (2009). Evaluation of mindful sport performance enhancement (MSPE): A new approach to promote flow in athletes. *Journal of Clinical Sport Psychology, 3*(4), 334–356. https://doi.org/10.1123/jcsp.3.4.334

Linley, A., & Bateman, T. (2018). *The strengths profile book: Finding what you can do + love to do and why it matters* (2nd ed.). CAPP Press.

Lomas, T. (2016). The dialectics of emotion. In *Second wave positive psychology : embracing the dark side of life* (pp. 5–30). London and New York: Routledge.

Mumford, G. (2016). *The mindful athlete : secrets to pure performance*. Parallax Press.

Saltzman, A. (2018). *A still quiet place for athletes : mindfulness skills for achieving peak performance & finding flow in sports & life*. New Harbinger Publications, Inc.

Salzberg, S. (2017). *Real love : the art of mindful connection*. Bluebird.

Schmeichel, B. J., & Baumeister, R. F. (2010). Effortful attention control. In B. Bruya (Ed.), *Effortless attention : A new perspective in the cognitive science of attention and action* (pp. 29–49). Cambridge and London: The MIT Press.

Sheldon, K. M., Prentice, M., & Halusic, M. (2015). The experiential incompatibility of mindfulness and flow absorption. *Social Psychological and Personality Science, 6*(3), 276–283. https://doi.org/10.1177/1948550614555028

Siegel, D. J. (2018). *Aware : The science and practice of presence - a complete guide to the groundbreaking wheel of awareness meditation practice*. Scribe Publications.

Swann, C., Crust, L., & Vella, S. A. (2017). New directions in the psychology of optimal performance in sport: flow and clutch states. *Current Opinion in Psychology, 16*, 48–53. https://doi.org/10.1016/J.COPSYC.2017.03.032

Tate, D. (2019d). *Mindful ascending for flowing descending: Can teaching alpine ski instructors mindfulness strategies foster more flow experiences on the slopes?* Buckinghshire New University.

Ullen, F., de Manzano, O., Theorell, T., & Harmat, L. (2010). The physiology of effortless attention: Correlates of state flow and flow proneness. In B. Bruya (Ed.), *Effortless attention : A new perspective in the cognitive science of attention and action* (pp. 205–217). Cambridge and London: The MIT Press.

Weber, R. (2019). The synchronization theory of flow: Neuropsychological evidence and the theory's future in the field of neuroaesthetics. In *Flow Symposium*. Frankfurt: Max Planck Institute for Empirical Aesthetics.

Wulf, G., & Lewthwaite, R. (2010). Effortless motor learning?: An external focus of attention enhances movement effectiveness and efficiency. In B. Bruya (Ed.), *Effortless attention : A new perspective in the cognitive science of attention and action* (pp. 75–101). Cambridge and London: The MIT Press.

Ziglar, Z. (1997). *Over the top: Moving from survival to stability, from stability to success, from success to significance* (Revised). Nashville, Atlanta, London, Vancouver: Thomas Nelson Publishers.

Chapter 11

Kaufman, S. B. (2018). Self-actualizing people in the 21st century: Integration with contemporary theory and research on personality and well-being. *Journal of Humanistic Psychology*, 1–33. https://doi.org/10.1177/0022167818809187

Kaufman, S. B. (2020). *Transcend: The science of self-actualization*. TarcherPerigee.

Maslow, A. H. (1943). A theory of human motivation. *Psychological Review*, 370–396.

Maslow, A. H. (1950). Self-actualizing people: a study of psychological health. *Personality, Symposium 1*, 11–34.

McAdams, D. P. (1993). *The stories we live by: personal myths and the making of the self*. New York and London: Guilford Press.

Moore, T. (2009). *A life at work: The joy of discovering what you were born to do*. Piatkus.

Peterson, C., & Seligman, M. E. P. (2004). *Character strengths and virtues: A handbook and classification*. American Psychological Association and Oxford University Press.

Tate, D. (2020e). Why do so few women become educators and examiners of snowsport instructors? Retrieved from https://www.paralleldreams.co.uk/post/why-do-so-few-women-become-examiners-of-snowsport-instructors

Chapter 12

Bao, K. J., & Schreer, G. (2016). Pets and happiness: Examining the association between pet ownership and wellbeing. *Anthrozoos, 29*(2), 283–296. https://doi.org/10.1080/08927936.2016.1152721

Capaldi, C., Passmore, H.-A., Nisbet, E., Zelenski, J., & Dopko, R. (2015). Flourishing in nature: A review of the benefits of connecting with nature and its application as a wellbeing intervention. *International Journal of Wellbeing, 5*(4), 1–16. https://doi.org/10.5502/ijw.v5i4.449

Ivtzan, I. (2015). *Awareness is freedom: The adventure of psychology and spirituality*. Winchester and Washington: Changemakers Books.

Ivtzan, I., Lomas, T., Hefferon, K., & Worth, P. (2016). *Second wave positive psychology: embracing the dark side of life*. London and New York: Routledge.

Kaufman, S. B. (2020). *Transcend: The science of self-actualization*. TarcherPerigee.

Keyes, C. L. M. (2002). The mental health continuum: From languishing to flourishing in life. *Journal of Health and Social Behavior, 43*(2), 207–222. https://doi.org/10.2307/3090197

Keyes, C. L. M. (2007). Promoting and protecting mental health as flourishing. *American Psychologist, 62*(2), 95–108. https://doi.org/10.1037/0003-066X.62.2.95

Rogers, C. (1959). A Theory of therapy, personality, and interpersonal relationships: As developed in the client-centered framework. In S. Koch (Ed.), *Psychology: A study of a science. Vol. 3: Formulations of the person and the social context* (pp. 184–256). New York: McGraw-Hill.

Seligman, M. E. P. (2011). *Flourish: a new understanding of happiness and well-being--and how to achieve them*. London and Boston: Nicholas Brealey Pub.

Tate, D. (2020d). Mental health vs. mental illness: Is the sporting world confused? Retrieved from https://www.paralleldreams.co.uk/post/mental-health-vs-mental-illness-is-the-sporting-world-confused

Chapter 13

Duckworth, A. (2016). *Grit: the power of passion and perseverance*. London: Vermilion.

Frankl, V. E. (2004). *Man's search for meaning: the classic tribute to hope from the Holocaust*. Rider.

Ivtzan, I. (2015). *Awareness is freedom: The adventure of psychology and spirituality*. Winchester and Washington: Changemakers Books.

REFERENCES

Ivtzan, I., Lomas, T., Hefferon, K., & Worth, P. (2016). *Second wave positive psychology : embracing the dark side of life*. London and New York: Routledge.

Kaufman, S. B. (2020). *Transcend: The science of self-actualization*. TarcherPerigee.

Lomas, T., Waters, L., Williams, P., Oades, L. G., & Kern, M. L. (2020). Third wave positive psychology: broadening towards complexity. *The Journal of Positive Psychology*, 1–15. https://doi.org/10.1080/17439760.2020.1805501

Macy, J., & Johnstone, C. (2012). *Active hope: How to face the mess we're in without going crazy*. Novato: New World Library.

McAdams, D. P. (1993). *The stories we live by : personal myths and the making of the self*. New York and London: Guilford Press.

Reivich, K., & Shatte, A. (2002). *The resilience factor: 7 keys to finding your inner strength and overcoming life's hurdles*. New York: Three Rivers Press.

Seligman, M. E. P. (2006). *Learned optimism: How to change your mind and your life*. New York: Vintage Books.

Seligman, M. E. P., & Csikszentmihalyi, M. (2000). Positive psychology: An introduction. *American Psychologist*, *55*(1), 5–14. https://doi.org/10.1037/0003-066X.55.1.5

Smith, E. E. (2017). *The power of meaning : The true route to happiness*. London, Sydney, Auckland, Johannesburg: RIDER.

Snyder, C. R. (2002). Hope theory: Rainbows in the mind. *Psychological Inquiry*, *13*(4), 249–275. https://doi.org/10.1207/S15327965PLI1304_01

Steger, M. F. (2012). Making meaning in life. *Psychological Inquiry*, *23*(4), 381–385. https://doi.org/10.1080/1047840X.2012.720832

Tate, D. (2020c). Hope: The fuel for strength and courage in challenging times. Retrieved from https://www.paralleldreams.co.uk/post/hope-the-fuel-for-strength-and-courage

REFERENCES

Wong, P. T. P. (2011a). Positive psychology 2.0: Towards a balanced interactive model of the good life. *Canadian Psychology/Psychologie Canadienne*, *52*(2), 69–81. https://doi.org/10.1037/a0022511

Wong, P. T. P. (2011b). Reclaiming positive psychology: A meaning-centred approach to sustainable growth and radical empiricism. *Journal of Humanistic Psychology*, *51*(4), 408–412. https://doi.org/10.1177/0022167811408729

Ziglar, Z. (1997). *Over the top: Moving from survival to stability, from stability to success, from success to significance* (Revised). Nashville, Atlanta, London, Vancouver: Thomas Nelson Publishers.

Ziglar, Z., & Ziglar, T. (2014). *Born to win: Find your sucess code*. Ziglar Inc.

ACKNOWLEDGEMENTS

There are so many people who have helped to make this book a reality.

Thank you to all those who contributed their thoughts about the various subjects covered, giving me quotes to use and permission to include a little of their stories; Nancy Chambers, Tania Cotton, Sharon Crossan, Martin Drayton, Robbie Fenlon, Kirst Galley, Hugh Monney, Dee O'Neill, Dave Ryding, David Smith MBE, Phil Smith, Shona Tate, Helen Trayfoot-Waugh, and Danny Ward. All of these real-life examples from true 'experts' has helped to bring the book alive and make it more meaningful for the reader.

Thank you to the members of the Irish Interski Demo Team who were the willing participants for my research and dissertation; Andy Bennett, Phil Brown, Jamie Kagan, John Paul McCarthy, Chris Oldaker, Jordan Revah, Mark Shaxted, Federico Sollini, Shona Tate and Lee Wright.

A special thanks to my dissertation supervisor, Dr. Genevieve Cseh, for her immense support and guidance. To all the staff at Bucks New University – MAPP course leaders (during my time on the course); Dr. Matthew Smith and Dr. Piers Worth and to the other lecturers; Dan Collinston, Lesley Lyle and Dr. Ceri Sims and visiting lecturers Alex Linley and Andrew Machon. And to the best cohort ever including; Inge Beckers, Ali Birch, Romyann Brooks, Tina Campbell, David Crane, Steve

Emery, Katherine Halliday, Lisa Jones, Sarah Monk, Nicola Morgan, Lee Newitt, Tracy Richardson, Siiri Saas, Eleonora Saladino and Sarah Smith to name a few. I learned so much from all of you and thanks to our monthly meet up calls online I am still learning so much from you.

To all those who have helped with reading the various drafts of this manuscript (and specific chapters) and offering their wise thoughts and editing ideas. In addition to the book contributors, already mentioned, thanks to Bernadette Callanan, Jane Campbell Morrison, Kat Congleton, Marit van Kampen, Sheelagh Lennon, Audrey Renton, Tracy Richardson and my brother Nigel Tate.

I would also like to mention all the eminent psychologists and/or meditation teachers that I have had the pleasure of meeting at conferences and/or corresponding with by email or social media; Dr. Mihaly Csikszentmihalyi, Dr. Barbara Fredrickson, Dr. Itai Ivtzan, Dr. Susan Jackson, Dr. Scott Barry Kaufmann, Dr. Tim Lomas, Sharon Salzberg, Dr. Michael Steger and Dr. Paul Wong. Their work and teachings have been of great influence on me.

Finally, I would like to thank my wife Shona, not only for her contributions to this work, but for always supporting me through whatever crazy projects I embark upon including this book!

INDEX

A
Active hope, 232–233
Agency thinking, 231, 235
Alpine Ski Leader, 149
Amotivation, 91–92
AQAL Integral Theory, 117
Arnold, John, 78
Ashworth, Sara, 28, 79, 121, 136
Auschwitz, 231
Australian Open – tennis, 22
Authentic self, 219
Autotelic, 155

B
Back country skiing, 32, 117
Baker, Philip, 103
Baltzell, Amy, 75, 169, 180–181, 184
Bao, Katherine Jacobs, 225
Base jumping, 140
Basketball, 35, 43, 66
Bateman, Trudy, 16, 90, 194
Baxter, Alain, 108
BBC Breakfast, 71
Beam of energy, 53, 66, 166
Becker, Boris, 151
Beckers, Inge, 73
Bespoke, 71
Bezos, Jeff, 15
Big air – snow sports, 140
Biochemistry, 49, 113
Boardercross, 203
Bobsleigh – winter sport, 108
Bond, James, 14
Boston University, 75
Branson, Richard, 15
Breadth of attention, 123, 193
Bryant, Fred, 107
Bryant, Kobe, 75
Bucks Fizz – pop group, 44
Bucks New Uni, 73
Buddhist, 72
Burnout – athlete, 25, 36
Burrows, Dave, 105

C
Caldwell, Tommy, 135
Campbell, Joseph, 23
Canoe coach, 118
Capaldi, Colin, 223
Carrick-Anderson, Emma, 19
Carrick-Smith boys, 19
Carving (skiing), 65
Cathcart, Stuart, 56
Catmull, Ed, 114
Cello – musical instrument, 116
Chambers, Nancy, 118
Chamonix Mont Blanc, 32, 95, 97–98, 117–118, 227
Character strengths, 16–17, 111, 194, 208–209, 237
Châtel, 116
Clubfoot, 108–109
Clutch state (mental), 185, 189
Cognitive dissonance, 38
Cognitive psychology, 51, 74
Comfort zone, 27, 29–30, 41, 43–45, 98, 141
Computing, 113
Concentration camp, 230
Coronavirus, 6, 90, 227, 235

Cotton, Tania, 119–120
COVID-19, 37, 64, 110, 220, 228–229, 231, 235–236
Cox, Richard H., 132
Coyle, Daniel, 29, 34–35, 44
Crossan, Sharon, 99–100
Cseh, Genevieve, 137
Csikszentmihalyi, Mihaly, 1, 38–39, 52–53, 115, 129–132, 136, 138–140, 146, 155
Curiosity, 6, 81–82
Cycling – road, 59, 108–110, 133–134, 151

D

Dachau, 231
Davis, Orin, 193–194
Dawn Wall, The, 135
Daydreaming, 54
Deci, Edward, 88–91
Decision-making, 114, 120, 124
Deep practice, 29, 35
Deliberate practice, 5, 26, 29–33, 35, 47–48, 78, 187
de Manzano, Orjan, 187
Dietrich, Arne, 58
Discovery threshold, 121
Dopamine, 156
Doran, George T., 27
Drayton, Martin, 202–205
Duckworth, Angela, 14, 86, 234
Dumont, Cedric, 141
Dweck, Carol, 21–22

E

Edberg, Stefan, 151
Ego, 9, 92, 195, 213, 217–220, 241
Ego concept, 219

El Capitan, 135
Emotions, 2–3, 86, 97, 108, 111–112, 115, 141, 156, 165, 170, 175–176, 216, 222, 224, 229
Endorphins, 156
Epstein, David, 19
Ericsson, Anders, 26–27, 29–31, 33, 35, 47–48, 78
European Flow Researchers Network (EFRN), 132
Eurosport, 149
Eurovision song contest, 44
Everest expedition, 117
Existential psychology, 240–241
Experiencing Sampling Method (ESM), 131
Explicit memory, 58–60
External focus – attention, 61–63, 65, 67–68, 77, 124, 135, 153, 187, 190
External rewards, 89
Extrinsic motivation, 6, 87–92, 156

F

Federer, Roger, 19, 132
Fenlon, Robbie, 117
Film producer, 119
Fitts, Paul, 39
Fixed mindset, 22–23, 34
Flourishing, 72, 216–217, 223
Form – manoeuvre-based, 77–78
Formula 1 (car racing), 68
Frankl, Viktor, 180–181, 230, 241
Fredrickson, Barbara, 13, 111, 115, 175

INDEX

Free solo – climbing, 135, 140
Freestyle skiing, 140
Freestyle snowboarding, 140
Function – skills-based, 77–78
Furlough, 71

G
Galley, Kirst, 97–98
Gates, Bill, 15
Generalise, 5, 13, 18–19
Gilbert, Daniel, 54
Goals – see long-term, task and session goals
Golf, 66, 151
Goodlad, Bruce, 98
Grand Prix de Monaco Historic, 66, 69
Grand Slam – tennis, 22
Gregoire, Carolyn, 54, 126
Grit, 14, 86, 234
Gritty hope, 234
Groundwater, Emma, 56, 160
Growth mindset, 21–23, 34

H
Half pipe – snow sports, 140
Hart, Rona, 74
Harvard University, 74
Hefferon, Kate, 2, 216, 240
Hematoma, 109
Herbert, Brian, 11
Highlining, 95, 140, 144
Hirscher, Marcel, 31
Holocaust, 230
Humanistic psychology, 1–3, 87
Human motivation, 6, 87–88, 209

I
Ideal self, 218
IFMGA mountain guide, 117
Imaginative play, 124
Implicit memory, 58–59
Inherent satisfaction, 91
Inspiration – emotion, 108, 115
Integral coach, 117
Interest – emotion, 13–15
Internal focus – attention, 61–68, 124, 135, 176, 187, 190
International Network on Personal Meaning INPM, 241
Intrinsic feedback, 18, 28, 78, 81, 123, 135–136, 192
Irish Interski Team, 162, 179, 193–194
Ivtzan, Itai, 2, 57, 72–74, 219, 223

J
Jackson, Susan A., 29, 131, 139, 159–160
Jobs, Steve, 15
Joffe, Peter, 114, 120–121, 124
Johnson, Andrew, 221
Johnstone, Chris, 232
Jordan, Michael, 75
Jorgeson, Kevin, 135
Joy – emotion, 86, 115
Jung, Carl, 130

K
Kabat-Zinn, Jon, 72, 74
Kahneman, Daniel, 186–187, 189
Karate, 32, 108, 200–201

Kaufmann, Scott Barry, 1, 34, 82, 126, 205, 209, 220, 240–241
Killingsworth, Matthew, 54
Kinaesthetic awareness, 28, 123, 134, 136
Kotler, Steven, 131

L
Langer, Ellen, 39, 74, 76–77, 80
Langerian mindfulness, 74
Lasting hope, 233, 235, 239
Learned optimism, 234
Learning contract, 42
Learning goals, 105
Lee, Bruce, 30, 32
Le Tour – ski area, 227
Lewthwaite, Rebecca, 62–64, 187
Linley, Alex, 16, 90, 194
Lockdown, 37, 90, 227–230, 235–236
Lockerbie, Andrew, 28, 79, 134
Loehr, James, 88
Logotherapy, 230–231
Lomas, Tim, 2, 57, 111, 159, 175, 216, 241
London 2012, 108–109
Long-term goals, 85–90, 93, 199, 201
Lyubomirsky, Sonja, 107

M
Macy, Joanna, 232
Majdanek, 231
Mandela, Nelson, 15
MAPP – MSc Applied Positive Psychology, 2–3, 39, 42, 56, 72–73, 75–76, 86, 91, 202, 222, 231
Maslow, Abraham, 1–2, 197, 199, 205, 209–210, 220
Mastery, 18–19, 25, 31, 35, 46–49, 85
Mastery goals, 105
MBSSI (Mindfulness based skiing specific intervention), 56–57, 73–76, 162–170, 173, 177–180, 184
McAdams, Dan P., 207, 240
McGonigal, Kelly, 122
McGregor, Alan, 32
McGregor, Matt, 56
Meaning – in life, 2, 9–10, 156, 181, 205–206, 227–228, 230–231, 239–241, 245
Meditation – types of, 72
Memmert, Daniel, 123–124
Mental health, 9, 88, 107, 213, 215–217
Mental illness, 9, 215–216
Mental strength, 141
Mental toughness, 100, 236
Mindful daydreaming, 54
Mindfulness – facets of, 56
Mindset – growth & fixed, 21–23, 34
Mind-wandering, 54–55
Moguls (skiing), 65, 151
Monney, Hugh, 37
Mont Blanc, 95, 97–98
Monte Carlo, 66
Moodymanc, 67
Moore, Thomas, 205
Moran, Aidan P., 51, 53, 124
Moser-Pröll, Annemarie, 150
Mosston, Muska, 28, 79, 121, 136

INDEX

Motor learning, 43, 61–63, 65, 78, 123–125, 132
Motor racing, 66
Movement analyst, 119
Mt. Ventoux, 109–110
Mumford, George, 75, 131, 170, 181
Murray, Andy, 22
Musician, 34, 46, 61, 67–68, 118, 137
Myelin, 29

N
Neuroscientist, 58
Neurotransmitter, 156
Non-judgemental, 72, 177
Novelty, 17, 81, 88

O
O'Neal, Shaquille, 75
O'Neill, Dee, 95–97
Open/closed sports, 43, 45, 65, 77
Optimal experience, 46, 129, 150, 164
Optimal performance, 184
Optimism, 9, 233–235
Organismic integration theory (OIT), 90
Oxytocin, 156

P
Pamporovo – ski area Bulgaria, 24, 152, 162, 167, 175, 179, 195, 228
Pandemic, 6, 64, 71, 110, 148, 220, 228–229, 231, 235
Paralympics, 108
Pathways thinking, 231, 235
Performance analysis, 33, 153, 173
Performing arts, 116, 126
Perry, Fred, 22
Perseverance, 86
Peterson, Christopher, 111, 208
Photographer, 119
Physical distancing, 229
Physical education (PE), 100, 200
Pixar, 114
Plake, Glen, 32
Posner, Michael, 39–40
PP 2.0, 2, 216
Preparation zone (learning), 41–43, 141
Preparatory zone (new flow model), 189–190, 192
Pride – emotion, 108, 115, 204, 218–219
Problem solve, 79, 81
Proprioception, 123, 134
Psychological needs, 88
Psychological well-being, 107, 215

R
Realised strengths, 90
Red Bull athlete, 141
Resilience, 2, 100, 110, 236–238
Rigorous practice, 30, 200, 202
Rio 2016, 109–110, 133
Rock climbing, 95, 135, 140, 154
Rogers, Carl, 1–2, 218
Rowing, 108–109
Russo-Netzer, Pninit, 73
Ryan, Richard, 88–91
Ryding, Dave, 37

S

Sailing, 118
Saltzman, Amy, 75–76, 132, 184
Salzberg, Sharon, 172, 221
Savouring, 2, 106–108, 112
Schneider, Verni, 150
Schooler, Jonathan, 55
Schreer, George, 225
Second wave PP, 2, 216, 240
Self-actualisation, 1, 3, 199, 209–210, 220–221, 239
Self-check – teaching style, 28, 136
Self-compassion, 2
Self-concept, 40, 46, 195, 218
Self-determination theory, 88, 90
Self-determined behaviour, 88, 91
Self-esteem, 218
Self-image, 218
Self-motivation, 88–89
Self-pity, 229
Self-regulation, 160
Self-transcendence, 220–221
Self-worth, 89, 92
Seligman, Martin, 1, 86, 111, 208, 216, 234, 240
Sense of control, 150–151, 166, 186, 237
Separable outcome, 89, 91–92
Serotonin, 156
Session goals, 27, 42, 133, 232
Shafir, Rebecca, 57
Sheldon, Kennon, 160
Shiffrin, Mikaela, 31, 133, 150
Shinty – Scottish Gaelic sport, 108
Short-term memory, 120
Siddique, John, 221
Side-cut (skiing), 65
Siegel, Dan, 170, 184
Sinek, Simon, 235
Skidding (skiing), 64–65
Ski Sunday (BBC2), 149
Ski touring, 95, 98, 201, 224
Slacklining, 140
Slopestyle – snow sports, 140
Smith, David, 108–112, 237
Smith, Emily Esfahani, 240
Smith, Matthew, 42
Smith, Phil, 20, 45, 77
Snowsport Scotland, 149
Snyder, Charles, 231, 235
Social distancing, 229
Social psychology, 87
Solo climbing, 135, 140
Spanish flu, 228
Specialise, 5, 13, 18
Spirituality, 202
Sports psychology, 75–76
Stand up paddle boarding, 140
Steger, Michael, 239–241
Stenmark, Ingemar, 31
Storytelling, 240
St. Patrick's Day, 228
Stretch zone, 27, 29, 41, 44–45, 98, 141
Summers, Joshua, 75, 169, 180–181, 184
Swann, Christian, 131, 184, 189
Syed, Matthew, 19, 35
Synchronised skiing, 163–164, 173, 185, 193

INDEX

T
Tactics, 114, 124
Task goals, 105, 133–134, 142–143, 232
Tate, Shona, 117, 123
Taylor, Jim, 105
Teaching styles, 79, 121, 136
Team GB, 108–110
Team Ireland, 228
Tennis, 19, 22, 66, 151
The Herald – newspaper, 110
Third wave PP, 241
Ticher, Tommy, 200
Time transformation, 154–155, 183
Tour du Mont Blanc, 95
Track athletics, 48, 108
Trail running, 95–97, 101
Transcendence, 209, 220, 240–241
Transient hypofrontality, 58
Trayfoot-Waugh, Helen, 116

U
Ullen, Fredrik, 187
University College Dublin, 51
University of Aberdeen, 78
University of Bath, 110
University of Pennsylvania, 86
UTMB, 95, 97

V
Van Avermaet, Greg, 133
van den Hout, Jef, 193–194
Veroff, Joseph, 107
Virtues, 208–209
Vonn, Lindsay, 51, 150

W
Walrave, Bob, 193–194
Wapnick, Emilie, 20
Ward, Danny, 67–68
Wilber, Ken, 117
Williams, Jane, 98
Wilson, Hersch, 27
Wilson, Larry, 27
Wimbledon – Grand Slam tennis, 22, 150
Wingsuit flying, 95, 140–141
Wisdom, 2, 209
Wong, Paul, 241, 268
Working memory, 120
World Championships – sports, 49, 109, 203
World Interski – congress, 3, 152, 162, 179, 190, 193–194, 228
Worth, Piers, 2, 42, 216, 240
Wulf, Gabriele, 62–64, 187

Y
Yosemite National Park, 135

Z
Ziglar, Zig, 21, 87, 170, 228, 234, 238
Zurbriggen, Pirmin, 32

THOUGHT CLOUDS COLLATED

Knowing your strengths can help you to discover what interests you most.

Genes, opportunity and skill are all part of the mix to becoming talented.

Speed masks accuracy but speed can also be your friend.

Mindful learning requires a mindful teaching approach where strategies are varied to suit the individual.

> Curiosity is at the heart of exploration which, in turn, promotes 'growth' as you learn.

> Passion provides the emotional fuel for maintaining your interests and driving you forward towards your goals.

> Keep embarking on new voyages, which involve lifelong learning, while living life in the present through being mindful, seeking flow and savouring.

> The way that you learn and the way that you are taught early on determine whether the seeds of creative performance are sown!

> Learning' is often an untidy process, but that is what makes it FUN. And that is what creates creativity!

> Over reliance on extrinsic feedback from a coach **inhibits** rather than facilitates flow.

> Flow experiences are filled with apparent paradoxes not least because they are based on people's subjective self-reports.

> Understanding what can inhibit flow is almost as important as understanding what can facilitate it.

- Practicing effortful attention in mindfulness can lead to, or encourage, effortless attention in flow.

- Having ALL FOUR flow foundations in place (rather than three) further increases the chances of experiencing flow.

- Let your interests shape your purpose over the passage of time.

- A values-based purpose will lead to exhibiting many of the characteristics of the self-actualised person.

> Good mental health is about moving from 'zero to flourishing' and finding time to simply be is an important part of the process.

> Lasting hope requires you to; **pause** and reflect, **be** present, **decide** on your intention, then **do**. Lasting hope is grounded in reality.

ABOUT THE AUTHOR

Derek Tate, MAPP is a positive psychology practitioner, flow coach and alpine ski teacher. He has spent the last 34 years teaching people of all ages and abilities to ski, including training and examining ski instructors for several national governing bodies/training organisations. As a PG Sports Coaching graduate of Moray House, Edinburgh in 1992 he has always been passionate about how people learn and the psychology of learning. This led to more recent studies and research when he embarked on the MSc Applied Positive Psychology (MAPP) at Bucks New University graduating with distinction in 2019. His passion for writing has developed over this time and involved coaching manuals, student resources and books all related to teaching and learning. He regularly writes blogs for the Parallel Dreams Coaching Academy.

Derek currently spends much of his time, with his wife, in Saint Gervais les Bains where they run British Alpine Ski School Chamonix and Megève over the winter months. When he is not coaching, he loves to get out walking in the mountains with his dogs.

YOUR NOTES, THOUGHTS & IDEAS

YOUR NOTES, THOUGHTS & IDEAS

Printed in Great Britain
by Amazon